The Covenant Connection

To the Gospel Internet. Learn how to Access Your Record in Heaven

Larry Ben Stephens, Sr.

Also Known As "Uncle Larry"
By Students Of
Forest Lake Academy
1968-1999

EDITED BY

WANDA BRACE HOPKINS

Florida Hospital College
Forest Lake Academy

SECOND EDITION

ISBN: 9780982947609

Library of Congress Control Number: 2010938966

Published by
NewBookPublishing.com, a division of Reliance Media, Inc.
2395 Apopka Blvd., #200, Apopka, FL 32703
NewBookPublishing.com

Printed in the United States of America

Reliance
Media

Dedication

To Libby,

Libby believed in me when I was less than nothing: no job, no money, no education. After fifty six years she still believes. Amazing!

And Wanda Brace Hopkins. Not only is she a fabulous friend, but if not for her encouragement, expertise, and support this book would never have seen the light of day.

Table of Contents

Introduction

In working with the Covenant over the last forty-nine years, I have seen our amazing Jesus intervene so many times in lives as the result of prayer, interventions that have left me dumbfounded, rubbing my eyes in disbelief. I'll start with two.

The Storm

As a married student with two small children, work and study left little time for my family except on Sabbaths. Very close to the campus of what is now Southern Adventist University is a small park called, appropriately enough, Student Park. One Sabbath afternoon my family and I were walking toward this park when we were overtaken by a sudden, fast-moving, violent thunderstorm. We sought shelter under a large tree, but soon the rain worked through the leaves. Looking toward the park, I saw rock cliffs. At the base of those cliffs was a depression that receded far enough to get us out of the downpour. My wife and I picked up our son and daughter and ran for safety. Sure enough, we were out of the rain and lightning, but the temperature was dropping rapidly. Our daughter Debby was four at the time, and looking up at me, she asked, "Daddy, let's ask Jesus to stop the rain; I'm cold!"

I replied we certainly could. As we knelt on the ground, even before the first word of Debby's prayer, I knew she was in for a disappointment. That rain was coming down in sheets, harder than ever. I had already decided what to tell her; it was so simple! We needed to go home because we were cold, but the starving people in China needed food. Jesus had to decide whether to stop the rain for us or let it keep raining so the farmers could grow more food for those starving Chinese children! As I had known, after her amen, she could hardly see the trees just a few feet outside our shelter.

I was ready with my little story when I looked into my daughter's eyes. The look she returned changed everything immediately, drastically. For the first time I saw doubt cloud her features. Doubting me was one thing, but there was no way I could allow mistrust of Jesus to develop in my child's mind. Her next words were, "Why didn't Jesus stop the rain, Daddy?"

Just that week in worship we had recounted the story of Joshua and the people of Israel crossing the Jordan River. I had emphasized that the waters of the river would not part until the priests with the Ark of the Covenant stepped into the water. They had to demonstrate faith by their action. I directed my daughter to remember this worship thought, and then I asked "Debby, we didn't show we believed Jesus would stop the rain, did we?"

With a puzzled expression, she countered, "How can we do that, Daddy?"

I replied, "Let's pray again and this time when we are finished, we'll go home." As Debby petitioned Jesus, her mother and I silently joined in. The storm wasn't our concern; it was the preservation of our child's faith. Prayer was over, and the storm had not abated. Joining hands, we walked toward the entrance. There are four witnesses to what happened. As we left the shelter, there may have been a few drops of rain fall on us; I don't recall any. Directly before us was brilliant sunlight. The storm continued to the right and left. Looking up, we saw a large horseshoe-shaped depression in the cloud above. I don't know that I have ever seen an angel, but I have seen their work so often. Coincidence?

The Ten-Dollar Bill

A few years later, I was teaching in Tallahassee, Florida. As with so many families with a tight budget, occasionally there was more month than money. Due to some unexpected expense, we were in that situation one Sunday morning. I happened to mention this to the family before worship as a precaution that we needed to be very careful until payday. Debby was to spend the day with one of her friends, and soon that family stopped by to pick her up. She was to return that evening. Later that day, I was to run an errand across town. On a lonely road a few miles from home, a small piece of paper blew across just ahead of my car. Now, I knew that wasn't money, but it was the right shape, and my favorite color, green, so I stopped. Walking back, I found a ten-dollar bill. There were no houses near and no cars on the road, so I placed the bill in my wallet. With a heartfelt prayer of thanksgiving, I continued on my business. Ten dollars certainly doesn't seem like much, but I knew it would be just enough to get us by.

That night Debby returned, and our family was together again. There had been no contact with our daughter since that morning. I asked her, "Debby, guess what I found today?"

The child looked at me, never so much as batted an eye, and replied, "Daddy, you found ten dollars."

Rapidly reviewing in my mind the day's activities, I knew there was no way she could have known. Very perplexed, I asked, "Young lady, how did you know I found that money?"

Again, with the nonchalance of a child to whom this was certainly no big deal, she replied, "As we were having worship this morning, I asked Jesus to help you find ten dollars."

Coincidence? The way Jesus has answered the prayers

of children removes coincidence from the realm of possibility. The adult mind can't help wondering if that child had been familiar with the value of the steps on the monetary ladder just how far up Jesus would have been willing to go. One hundred? One thousand? One …? The mind of a child doesn't deal in the philosophical. I'm sure the Holy Spirit impressed her to request that morning just what was adequate; that's His way.

Such simple, little things: sunlight in a storm; ten dollars. Yes, simple, little things make big impressions. I invite you to go with me on a journey, a journey with stops along the way for brief glimpses of the power and majesty of Jesus as He changed lives through prayer. Prayer that saved lives, took life, saved souls, and made the impossible possible.

My forty-nine years of ministry have involved three distinct phases: as a teacher and counselor of Adventist youth; as a pastor; and now as a hospice chaplain. My purpose in writing this book is to demonstrate that once people enter into God's Covenant, no matter what endeavor God leads them to, it becomes directed by His love, His guidance, **His Power!**

If you are not familiar with the terms of God's Covenant, if you are doubtful about your salvation, or even may think it is impossible to know without a shadow of a doubt that you are saved, if the only reason you bought this book was to learn how to access your heavenly record, turn to chapter seven and gain this assurance before continuing.

The first chapter describes my own struggle in accepting this assurance.

(Chapters 1 through 9 cover the subjects listed on the back cover; chapters 10 and 11 address concerns unique to the Seventh-day Adventist church.)

Chapter One

From Impossible To Possible

"You don't get a second chance to make a first impression." I believe I heard this in a shampoo commercial; I'm so very thankful God pays no attention to advertisement.

During the years I knew my father, he was not a professed Christian. At one time he had been a firm member of the Adventist church, a "worker" in our denomination, a Christian. Somehow, a misunderstanding had occurred, resulting in false accusations. Anger resulted in loss of temper, then coldness. Dad not only left the church, he left Jesus. He always mentioned the church with respect, but with deep sadness. Having said that, I have never known a more Christ-like man. Well respected in our community, one of those who would "give his shirt off his back," he was a soft touch for anyone in need. He may not have been a Christian, but he was "God" to me. Having been born late to my parents, my siblings had left home when I came on the scene. My father and I were together every chance we had, and most Sundays would find us on some lake fishing.

Dad taught me so much from simple things. I took some fishing line from our tackle box that seemed hopelessly tangled. Dad watched as I fingered it for a few seconds in utter frustration. "Looks hopeless, doesn't it, son?" he asked. I didn't reply, but he could see I was whipped. He took it from me and untangled a foot or two, then said, "Just take your time; work it out a knot or tangle at a time. It will come around." I did as he said, and he was right. So many times I have faced problems that seemed so complex, and that experience comes to mind, along with Dad's admonition, "Just take your time; work it out a knot or tangle at a time. It will come around."

I'm sure my parents had to draw on deep reserves of patience the day I nearly burned down our town. The war (WWII) was finally winding down, and in a war film there was a scene of a boat hit by a torpedo. Oil was burning on the water around the sinking ship. Humphrey Bogart dove in and swam underwater until he was beyond the burning. I was no more than eight years old, and this scene really bugged me. Oil can't burn on water! Humphrey Bogart was a phony!

As I walked home after the film, I noticed that a pool of water from a recent rain had collected in the street in front of our house. About three blocks up the street was the Moody Chevrolet Dealership. In the back of their repair shop were barrels cut in half where waste oil and gas were deposited.

This waste material was eventually carried away of course, but the rain had caused the contents of those barrels to overflow. Whatever was in them was coating the surface of the water along the street curb all the way down to our house. Oil on water! I could check out Humphrey Bogart myself! It was a bad thing to lose confidence in Humphrey Bogart!

I went into the house and found some matches. Needless to say my parents were gone. I struck one match and dropped it on the water's surface, nothing! I knew it! But Humphrey Bogart deserved another chance. I found some newspaper, wadded it up, lit it, and threw it on the surface of what I am now convinced contained a healthy dose of gasoline. My faith in Humphrey Bogart was immediately, drastically restored! Flames shot up over fifteen feet high and began burning a large oak tree on the corner. Then the fire began marching up the street toward the Moody Chevrolet Dealership!

To say I was petrified comes nowhere close to describing my reaction. On one hand, I wanted so much to stay and watch what I was sure would be the greatest fireworks show Texas had ever seen when that fire entered the back of the Moody Chevrolet Dealership. On the other hand, I was convinced the first adult who found out what I had done would probably skin me alive! I ran into the house and hid in a closet.

I could hear the sirens of the fire trucks that were stationed between our house and the Moody Chevrolet Dealership (lucky for the Moody Chevrolet Dealership). I actually can't remember anything beyond this except being found in the closet by my father. Everything else was probably erased by the trauma of having Humphrey Bogart's veracity vindicated!

My mother stayed faithful to the church and attended services every opportunity she had, even though the nearest church was thirty-five miles from our East Texas home. She certainly cared for me every bit as much as my father did, and she tried her best to engender in me love for Jesus and the church. Being the only Adventist in the county made that no easy task. High school football in Texas is an icon that dominates Friday nights. Sabbath observance and sports were constantly at odds in our home.

It was indelibly impressed on me at an early age the possible consequences of being a Seventh-day Adventist. One Sabbath when I was nine years old, my mother and I returned from church and after lunch I went out to play. Not far from our house I was confronted by several older boys and asked where I had been that day. I replied, "Church," which was immediately met with derisive laughter. Next I was questioned why anyone would go to church on Saturday. Was I a Jew? As any child would, I searched my mind to come up with an answer. I don't recall what I came up with, but I'll never forget the response. The first blow came from behind. In the next moments I was beaten and kicked to near unconsciousness. Finally, someone across the street saw what was happening and rushed to my aid. My attackers ran as I was picked up from the street. I learned that being an Adventist was far different from what I had previously realized. It was more than not attending football games on Friday nights. The struggle between my father's view of Jesus and the church and my mother's had begun. As for me, I was determined to play football--Friday nights or not.

The East Texas of my youth was rolling hills with streams and rivers in the valleys, dotted here and there with lakes and ponds. The forests seemed to go on forever. We lived on the edge of what Texans refer to as the Big Thicket, swamp and forest stretching from the Gulf coast almost to Oklahoma. I'm afraid education wasn't very high on my priority list. My rifle, dog, and fishing gear were.

One day, Paul, my best friend, and I were hunting close to a stream called Big Cypress when we discovered an abandoned sorghum press. Sorghum is a maize-like plant from which the juice is extracted by a press powered by a mule tethered to the end of a ten-foot pole. The mule goes in a circle as fresh sorghum stalks are fed into the rollers of the press. The juice is then piped into a large metal vat where it is boiled down to the thick, strong syrup known as sorghum molasses, an East Texas favorite with hot biscuits and butter. Our interest in the press was that vat. If not rusted, a few holes could be patched up, creating a fair facsimile of a boat. Paul and I soon had the vat repaired and were poling it up Big

Cyprus when we saw that a small tree had fallen across the creek during a recent storm. We soon found that jumping on the middle produced an excellent facsimile of a diving board, and that by jumping in unison we could go higher and higher. During one of those jumps we lost our balance. Paul fell forward, and as I began to fall backward, I decided to dive in that direction. Paul was pulling me out of the water as I regained consciousness. A sandbar had washed in during that storm and was only two or three inches beneath the surface when I dove into it. A terrible pain was centered in my neck, and I couldn't move my head. (When I think of the ignorance of those two kids, I shudder.) I maneuvered my head with my hands until I found a position that lessened the pain, and then asked Paul to help me up. We walked over a mile back to the house, then began a thirteen-mile trip to the hospital on a flat bed truck. Weeks of traction were followed by months of wearing a steel and leather contraption to hold my head straight. My dreams of football greatness were over.

Mom had always had a dream that one day I would attend a Seventh-day Adventist school. As my freshman year in high school approached, I heard more and more talk of academy. Finally, Dad agreed, and plans for my attendance at the academy in Keene, Texas, were made. It seemed like a neat idea. Keene was even called the Holy City by some in Texas, and I was sure students who attended there just needed a little brushing off before translation (being taken to heaven without experiencing death, like Enoch and Elijah.)

The Sunday I left, my father and I made plans for a fishing trip to our favorite lake the first time I returned. With tears we embraced, then Dad stood by the road as we left. It is approaching sixty years since that parting, but I'll never forget his face. The next Sunday, my first away from home, I received a call from my sister. Dad had gotten up to shave, collapsed on the floor, and died of a massive heart attack, as they say. I could never in a thousand years describe on these pages what that loss meant. The world I had known no longer existed, and I would never hunt or fish in East Texas again. When I arrived home, not only was my father gone, but my dog Corky was gone as well. Somehow that dog knew where Dad had been taken and was guarding the back door of the funeral home. He didn't bother anyone, but refused to return home until the hearse left for the cemetery. Dad was interred in our family plot 150 miles away. I'm convinced if we had buried him in town, Corky would have found the spot and continued his vigil; he and my father were that close. As it was, he gave the greatest demonstration of animal loyalty I've ever witnessed.

I returned to school from the funeral in a daze. Weeks passed and in November, our first Week of Prayer was held. It seemed the speaker offered hope, and at the end of the Friday night service, I made my way to him. I asked him how I could know Jesus; his answer was to change my life.

He said, "Young man, I'm busy right now, but if you want to know Jesus, just find a place all by yourself and pray for Him to make Himself known to you. And He will!"

It sounded so simple. I walked out of the auditorium into a clear, cold, star-studded Texas night and left campus. Continuing down "Old Betsy" road, I came to a field, walked to the center, and knelt in the dirt. I had no idea what I was doing, but I prayed for Jesus to make Himself known, as the man had said. Then I waited. Nothing. It was getting so cold. I waited some more. Nothing. Waited. Nothing. I looked into those brilliant Texas stars. Maybe I was supposed to see something. Nothing. Finally, I made three decisions in that Texas dirt. First, Dad was right: Jesus didn't exist. Second, that preacher was the biggest liar that ever wore shoes. Third, I didn't know if there was a hell or not, but as soon as I got back to campus, I intended to raise all I could until there was a chance to find out. The name, Jesus, was to be just another expletive.

I write this now as a pastor, teacher, and professional Christian counselor over seventy years old. Certainly, I hold no resentment toward that Week of Prayer speaker. I realize now, as I never could have then, the pressure he was under. I also know there must have been a Christian somewhere close I could have been directed to who could have personally led me to the Master. Satan was waiting for that boy who walked out of the field that night. I am so thankful for God's tenacity!

I didn't learn much in school the rest of that year. I found friends who were no more ready for translation than I was. Soon alcohol and tobacco were readily available through village contacts, and every opportunity was taken to leave campus and really learn in Fort Worth or Dallas. Our dormitory pranks convinced the boys' dean he had chosen the wrong profession, and before the year was over, he left.

That summer Mom obtained work in southern California, and the next fall I enrolled in La Sierra Academy. Soon I became part of a gang roaming the streets of our area, stealing anything not nailed down. We all attended the same school, worked in the daytime, operated at night. We found a "fence" (one who buys stolen goods) in Corona, California, who would purchase all the tires, batteries, and other merchandise we could provide. Siphoned gas was used for excursions into Los Angeles on weekends. Our favorite target became the California Department of Transportation, who regularly parked their equipment at job sites over the weekend. It became increasingly hard to get all that machinery working Monday mornings.

Christmas time was approaching during my junior year, and I needed holiday money. In order to supply it, I began a poker concession in an unused room in the back of the La Sierra gymnasium. All went well until a faculty member walked in and saw money and cards on the table. The principal took hardly any time at all explaining to me my presence was no longer desired. I was expelled. Immediately, I went home, threw some clothes in a bag, and hitchhiked out of California. The California Highway Patrol had been getting too close anyway.

I was sixteen years old, away from religion, through with education, and back in Texas. A few days with friends and I had located construction work. With my first paycheck, I rented a small apartment. Two more weeks, and I purchased my first car. Nothing fancy, but at sixteen and with my own pad and wheels, I had the world by the tail and in two months, sold my first car and bought a faster one.

I may have forgotten that November night in the dirt two years before. But Jesus hadn't. He had been steadily moving my life His way, and now He was ready to get serious. I was working on a four-story building and had climbed down to find my foreman. Walking around a corner, I heard a worker above yell, "Look out!" He was on top of the building and had for some reason thrown an unused bucket of fresh brick mortar over the side. I looked up just in time to receive that mortar full in the face. The force of the mixture was so great both eyeballs were completely impacted, and the quick lime it contained began eating away my flesh. Workers hurried to my side, led me to a faucet, and began trying to flush out the sand and cement. Water only activates lime more. The tool room foreman heard the commotion, looked out his window, and realized what had happened. For some reason he had a small amount of carbonic acid in a bottle by that window. Grabbing the container of acid, he ran to me and pushed the others aside. Knowing he only had enough to possibly save one eye, he carefully washed the cornea of my right eye with the acid, neutralizing the lime. Later, when he visited me in the hospital, he broke down sobbing as he apologized for not having had more acid. I have him and the Power that directed him to thank for the eyesight I have today. The road to the hospital was blocked by a freight train, causing a fifteen-minute delay. The doctor who worked on me said later that by the time he had cleaned out the mortar, my eyes looked like raw hamburger meat. He had doubted I would ever see again.

Eyes tightly bandaged, I was led to a room and told by a nurse to put on a hospital gown. I replied, "Lady, I can't see you, but I'll guarantee if you try to put that thing on me, you're in for the fight of your life!"

She hurried off to find help. The same Paul who had rescued me at Big Cypress had driven my car to the hospital and was in the room. I told him to go to my apartment, get clean clothes and my dress boots, and be sure to be back before that nurse. She returned with two doctors to find me on the bed in clean shirt, jeans and those boots, ready to fight. They all stood there for a moment, till finally one of the doctors asked, "Do you intend to stay like that in this hospital?"

I replied in the affirmative, and he turned to the nurse

and said, "Leave him alone!"

My bravado didn't last long in the blackness, alone. If there was a God, I begged Him to let me see. Two weeks later, the final bandages were removed, and I could see out of my right eye; the left was as white as a sheet. I was offered an ambulance ride but replied my car was in the parking lot, and I could manage on my own. As I left the hospital and stepped outside, the sunlight blinded those ravaged eyes so severely I almost fell. Groping along, I finally found the car and began to drive. Every few hundred yards it was necessary to pull over for a few minutes to rest. It seemed to take forever to get home.

Two weeks later my eyes still hadn't healed, but I refused to return to a doctor; they would be okay. On my way to south Texas to see a friend, I started to pass a truck on a bridge. My speed had been between seventy-five and eighty miles an hour. The biggest horse in Jasper County, Texas, stepped from in front of that truck into my lane. The collision threw the horse into the air and down on top of my car, crushing it almost to the seats. There was no longer a front end to that vehicle; with no control, I hit the bridge. By this time I was somewhere under the dash as my "pride and joy" was being dismantled. It finally ground to a halt, and I was able to crawl out a broken window. That car was now an almost unrecognizable hunk of steel with torn-off parts littering the bridge, here a fender, there a wheel. As I surveyed that wreckage I recalled a Bible class and a discussion over what would happen if a person suddenly found himself in a situation in which he knew there was no alternative but death. If asked at that moment, would God accept such an individual? I wondered where I would have been if I had died in that car. Was there really nothing beyond the grave? There was no way I could have avoided that mortar or the horse. Was someone trying to get a message to me? Who? What? I wasn't ready, yet, to pursue that further. My brother lived not far away and came to pick me up.

That horse ended up saving my sight. My mother was nursing at Loma Linda and had returned to work after visiting me in the hospital. Someone called to inform her of my continuing eye problems. She began asking the hospital staff if there was help for my condition. Doctor Louis George of San Bernardino, California, was suggested. Contacting Dr. George revealed he had developed a treatment for my type of injury. There is no way I would have returned to California as long as that car was around. Its demise made it much easier to logically conclude I was in trouble and better get help. After an examination, Dr. George told me if I had waited much longer, no one could have saved my sight.

For the next four months I was an outpatient receiving daily treatment. Worker's compensation was picking up the tab and sending a check for living expenses. With insurance money, time, and no direction, I spent both time and money gambling and working on my alcohol habit. My eyes finally healed. Scar tissue joined both eyeballs to their sockets in several places, but eye movement wasn't affected. I could even see a little out of the left eye, and it was no longer white. Dr. George hadn't released me, but that relentless drive to return to the road was getting stronger. To this day I have no idea what I had expected to find. Something was out there, somewhere, somehow, and I had to meet it!

Answering a classified ad turned up a gentleman running a magazine subscription scam. It made little difference to me what he was doing. It sounded like money, and he was heading in the right direction, east. Two days later five of us were in his station wagon headed for Arizona. I was now a con artist, a real flim-flam man. Supposedly a medical student searching for help to cover the tremendous cost of school, folks could "vote" for my success by purchasing subscriptions. Each of us had different scams, but the result was the same: we got money and quickly left town. It came as no surprise we were persona non grata-- escorted out of Albuquerque, New Mexico, thrown into jail in Las Vegas, New Mexico (Yes, friend, there is a Las Vegas in New Mexico). By the time we arrived in Dodge City, Kansas, I was six hundred miles from Dallas and had had enough. A black jack game in the Dodge City Hotel, a few hands, a little money, and I had caught a ride south.

Things were different in Texas. The economy was

down, and jobs were hard to find. In the search for work, the state was criss-crossed. It seemed nothing lasted; jobs kept playing out. It might be construction, hauling hay, janitorial; the days turned into a hot blur. Sometimes staying with friends, maybe a night keeping a trucker awake, occasionally a flophouse where for seventy-five cents or a dollar, a cubicle with a bed was provided; the night might mean a long walk with a nap here and there on a bench or in an unlocked car. Hunger became too familiar too often. For all intents and purposes, I had become a bum.

You must learn to read people on the street. In that jungle the smartest, quickest, or strongest survive. Having said that, I never got over the unwarranted kindness of so many who were considered society's outcasts or downtrodden.

One night a ride ended in a small East Texas oil town at midnight. Nothing was moving. There would be no ride out that night. A young prostitute saw me standing under a streetlight and walked over. After determining I had no money for her services, she said, "It's too dangerous for you on this street. Come with me, and I'll find a place for you to stay." (Too dangerous for me! That child was no more than eighteen years old and practicing one of the most dangerous professions on earth!)

Fearful that what she was really offering was an invitation to a mugging, I was constantly on guard as she led me down alleys and between houses. Finally, she approached a door and knocked. A middle-aged woman responded, and a short conversation ensued that I couldn't hear. I was invited in and shown to a bed. I'll never know how she did it, but I'll always be grateful.

So many times a ride would end on one side of a city, making it necessary to walk to the other side of town to begin thumbing on a different road. A ride stopped in Oak Cliff, a suburb of Dallas, and I began such a walk. Trying a short cut resulted in getting lost. As I crossed some railroad tracks, a group of black men were unloading a boxcar. I approached one of them and asked directions. Upon granting my request, the man looked at me a moment and then asked, " Boy, when was the last time you ate?"

I told him I thought the day before but wasn't sure. He held out fifteen cents and said, "You're a long way from Highway 80; take this and catch a bus."

His clothes told me he wasn't much better off than I. My reply, "Man, I can't take your money. How could I ever find you to pay you back?"

Another piercing look from those tired, knowing eyes, and he said, "Son, it ain't a question of paying back!"

I took his money, thanked him, found a hamburger stand and enjoyed a fifteen-cent feast. Afterward I discovered he was right; it was a long walk to Highway 80.

As much as I loved Texas, I knew there must be better opportunities elsewhere. Finally, one of those short-time jobs paid enough for a bus ticket back to California. A few days at my mother's and I visited a Marine Corps recruiter, having decided if I were going to fight through life, it might as well be for pay. For some reason, we were required to pass two physicals; one by army regulations in Los Angeles, the other by Navy standards in San Diego. When it came time for the eye exam at both locations there was no trouble with the right eye; for the left I was only able to make out the big "E" at the top of the page. No one seemed to notice. On my eighteenth birthday I raised my hand and swore to defend the Constitution of the United States of America as a Marine. Boot camp awaited.

At Camp Pendleton, the Marine base at San Diego, and after receiving uniform, weapons and platoon assignment, we met the man who was to have absolute control of our bodies and souls: our drill instructor, Staff Sergeant Lawrence Valenzuela. The first time the company commander addressed us, we were told in no uncertain terms the only reason we were in the Corps was to become the world's best trained professional killers. Now, we all had the same name, Boot. From four-thirty in the morning until ten-thirty at night, we were to undergo the rigorous, often brutal exercises it takes to produce a Marine.

I learned so much in boot camp I still use today: teamwork, discipline, the determination to stick to a task until it's completed or you're dead, respect for others (drill instructors, or D.I.s, are the world's best at instilling this!) and, finally, respect for myself. I also learned you don't take on a D.I. The one time I tried (can you say, **BIG MISTAKE?!**) couldn't be called a fight, for I can't recall ever landing a punch! The man was much faster with his feet than anyone I had ever fought with their hands. The only thing I can remember about the episode is bouncing off a wall occasionally.

During boot camp we were given a choice each Sunday, to drill as every other day or go to church. My entire platoon was regular in church attendance; it was the only place to go to get rest. On one such occasion a young Navy chaplain gave the most effective sermon I've ever heard. For some reason I can't explain, my mind was receptive to the Holy Spirit's influence. The message was on the life of Jesus: a man of sorrows, acquainted with grief, a man who refused to sell us out, even at the cost of crucifixion, the Man-God, who is the only hope for our crazy world. Every point was hitting home. From that time on the Spirit never let up. God had led me to the Corps to hear that message. Through all I had experienced, my mother and my sister, especially, had kept me in their prayers. Both told me later they had almost given up hope when I entered the Corps. Funny how things work out.

Within a week of that church service, I was ordered to appear before a board of five Navy doctors. Their question,

"How did you get into the Marine Corps with only one eye?"

I told the truth and then experienced the type of eye exam that can't be faked. The next day I was called before them again and told my service to the Corps was to be terminated. A few days later, I received an Honorable Discharge and mustering out pay. I suppose out of sheer habit, I bought a bus ticket east.

By now, I had traveled that desert between the California and Texas borders so many times I could almost predict the next turn in the road. During the long night that followed on that bus, my mind could find no rest. It seemed my life was working against some impenetrable wall. My home, my every plan or desire had been snatched from me by death, accident, or circumstance. I thought I had found a place in the Corps and now that was gone. With no practical education, and that young chaplain's words repeating in my conscience, I kept asking myself, "Where am I going?"

In El Paso I bought a ticket going south, and in Laredo, one for a bus heading east again. By the time I reached Houston, I decided to continue to Lake Charles, Louisiana, the home of my brother Ray, a Seventh-day Adventist preacher.

Ray had more sense than to try to engage me in a religious discussion; it was evident his younger brother was deeply troubled. He knew of one of his church members who needed help putting in a rice crop and asked if I were interested in taking the job. I began working with Melvin Johnson of Kinder, Louisiana, and was invited to stay in his home. Melvin and Bertha had six children, four at home and two away at Adventist schools. As I worked with Melvin, I began reading him with that street knowledge mentioned earlier. He certainly had a quick temper if directions weren't followed or his equipment goofed up, but he was a good man. I sat in on worship with his family and began accompanying them to church.

Rice depends on water. Once irrigation started, common knowledge dictated you couldn't shut down your pump until just before harvest without irreversible damage to the crop. Melvin's pump was a constant witness to his faith. You could hear those big motors for miles from farms all around. Each Friday, just before sundown, Melvin walked out to the well house and turned the motor off. The silence told his neighbors Melvin and his family were celebrating another Sabbath.

A Friend

Glendon Sibley was teaching in the small Seventh-day Adventist school in Lake Charles, Louisiana. Each school day, Bertha drove her children 80 miles round trip on narrow, two-lane roads to Lake Charles to attend that school. Glen's love of nature drew him like a magnet to the 640 acres of the Johnson farm, which contained large sections of forest. I found that Glen was also from East Texas, having been raised 40 miles from my home. It didn't take long to strike up a friendship, and soon we were spending every free moment in the woods together, often accompanied by the Johnson children. For me, the smell, feel, freedom, excitement, and adventure of the forest and fields had a much-needed cleansing effect.

Glen had a shed in the back of his place where he used to keep injured animals and some he wished to either tame or observe for a while. There were several species of owls, hawks, and various other birds, plus a few small mammals and reptiles caged in the building. We were on a cattle ranch hunting snakes when Glen's dog, Brownie, ran up to us yelping with an unmistakable, strong smell. We knew he had been nosing around an old pile of lumber and taking off a few boards revealed a beautiful little spotted skunk. Glen asked if I had any idea how we might catch it. I informed him there was no problem; the situation was well in hand! Somewhere, sometime I had heard if you got a skunk to raise its tail, just before he brought his formidable deterrents into play, and reached in and grabbed that tail, the animal was rendered defenseless. With this bit of woods wisdom, I told Glen the plan. He was to get in front of the skunk, dance around a little and make faces. When the tail was raised, I would swoop in from the rear for the capture. By the way, Glen has a grin he will wear when he knows he is in for a particularly good time.

He was wearing this full bore as he asked, "Are you sure this will work?"

I assured him my information was foolproof. With that, Glen took his position and began his dance. I grabbed an old gunny sack and waited. Sure enough, with a quizzical look in Glen's direction, the skunk began stamping his little feet and raising that tail. My cue! Grabbing our prize, I raised him to eye level. At this juncture I wish to bear witness to the fact that not only is a skunk not hindered in any way by this maneuver from exercising his God-given ability to defend himself, but he really develops an indignant attitude toward anyone using it. He let me have it with both barrels. To smell a skunk from afar and to be enveloped in a cloud of his musk I can assure you are two distinctly different experiences. I held onto the little varmint and put him in the sack. Back at the house, Bertha had me take off my clothes, which the boys held out on sticks as far as possible to take outside to burn. After a bath in tomato juice, I was not quite so aromatic. The farm dogs thought I was great, but it was several days before I felt comfortable in human company. We never had a chance to tame that skunk. The little ingrate chewed his way out of the shed in a couple of days and escaped.

Southern Louisiana is bayou country and contains thousands of alligators. Glen and I were anxious to try our hands at capturing one. Avery Island is the home of Tabasco Sauce and in the bayous close to the plant are rookeries where multiplied thousands of pairs of egrets, herons, and other birds nest in the cypress trees and on platforms built out into the water. We heard that at nesting time alligators gathered to cruise under the rookeries, waiting for nestlings or eggs to fall into the water. When we arrived on the scene, we found our information had certainly been accurate. The trees and platforms were white with bird life, and sure enough, ominous black forms floated underneath, ready for a meal.

Neither of us knew the first thing about approaching an alligator, much less catching one. After a few minutes of surveying the scene, Glen asked, "How are we going to do this?"

As usual, I was prepared with a plan. There was a rickety old boat on shore. I told Glen I would borrow the boat, paddle out to the alligators, slap the water with the oar and yell, thus driving the alligators into a nearby nook in the bayou. A long two-by-four lay near the boat. Glen was to wait until the alligators were all bunched up and, as I brought the vessel close to shore, get the board under a small one and flip it into the boat, whereupon I would subdue it. It made sense to me to start small and work our way up. As Glen picked up his plank, he was wearing that grin.

Sure enough, as I began the noise, those alligators started moving toward the nook, all sizes from two feet to over ten. Why, they were responding just like cattle! My confidence grew as the shore neared. Glen was ready and placed the board under a three-footer. A mighty heave, and the animal and I were eye to eye in the boat! I tried first to pin down the tail, whereupon a rapidly snapping set of teeth assured me there had to be a better way. Next, I tried grabbing its jaws, but the tail nearly knocked me out of the boat! I retreated to one end of the boat, the alligator to the other and for a moment we eyed each other, deciding on our next move. I must admit, the animal's plan was far superior to mine. I had decided to jump in the middle of the beast and work out to both ends. I forgot to mention an alligator's amazing ability to jump. As we met again in the middle of the boat, that critter came off the bottom as if he had wings, mouth wide open, right at my head! I ducked to the side; aha, he missed! The problem was I was also on my way over the side and into the bayou. As I surfaced, all those animals I had driven into this nook, the little ones and the very large ones, each was bobbing up and down on the waves, just looking at me. The little alligator was still in the boat, watching me from over the side. They all seemed to be patiently waiting to see what I would come up with next. I looked to the shore for help from Glen, but several rows of reptiles separated us, and he could be of no assistance. I decided it was far better that I swallow my pride and leave the field of battle as soon as possible (also, I might add, while I still had enough extremities to execute this decision!). I swam straight to shore, slapping the snout of any surly beast that got in the way.

Years later, I would learn the call that can bring an alligator right out on the bank. The Miccosukee Seminole Indians in the Everglades would share with me the ingredient they use to attract "gators," marshmallows!

I owe Glen so much. At a time when I really needed Christian fellowship, he provided it in spades. He was never preachy, but what a friend! He and his wife Irene have been missionaries to Africa for over twenty-five years in our educational work. In our conversations from time to time, they have described their adventures. Glen had an important part in encouraging me to enter teaching.

Melvin's oldest daughter Libby returned home for spring break. We were busy in the field from sunup to dark, but each evening Libby and I would talk. When she returned to school, I told her mother I was going to marry her daughter. I almost caused the poor woman to have a heart attack! She tried her best to come up with a plan that would keep her daughter away for the summer but to no avail. Libby returned home. She began taking my lunch to me in the field. As she walked through that rice, her auburn hair sparkled in the sun. I had never seen anything so beautiful! Occasionally she would ride behind me on my tractor. Now, that may not sound so romantic, but just to have her close became increasingly important to me. It could also be very disconcerting; in other words, I was beginning to have real trouble keeping my mind on my business!

We were riding together one day when a sudden bump caused the muffler to fall off. I knew that thing was red hot, but, as I said, my mind was elsewhere. I immediately jumped down and grabbed it, just as quickly receiving a nasty burn. Now, you're thinking that was really dumb, right? Wrong! Libby took me back to the house, bandaged my hand, sat with me in the shade and spent the rest of the afternoon feeding me homemade ice cream. I was tempted to go out the next day and grab that muffler with the other hand!

I didn't know how Libby felt about me, but I knew I loved her. I also had too much respect for her to allow our relationship to deepen in my spiritual condition. The war for my soul became relentless. To surrender was against my nature. Allow another being to control my will? Jesus? I returned to Dallas for a weekend with old friends. Maybe that life hadn't been so bad. On Monday morning as I prepared to return to the farm, I took a good long look in the mirror. The image returning that look told me without a doubt my time was running out. Alcohol, fights, wrecks, accidents, that mixture couldn't go on forever. The Holy Spirit was bearing down. What was I going to do about Jesus? Now there was no getting away from that question, no rest. Later that week while disking a field, I couldn't fight it any longer. I threw the tractor out of gear, jumped down, knelt in the dirt, and asked Jesus to take my life. There were no bright lights, angels singing, voices heard. What did happen was far more significant; that simple request connected me to God's Covenant and there was peace. I was no longer at war, war with God or myself or anybody else. I knew whatever happened it would be all right; I was finally home. As tears fell on that fresh earth, I remembered another field and a cold November Texas night. It was so good to finally be home with Jesus.

I must admit, beyond this peace I was experiencing, I had no real knowledge of what had actually taken place. It would be years before an in-depth study of the conversation between Jesus and Nicodemus as recorded in John' gospel would reveal that at that moment of acceptance, I was given everlasting life (John 3:16); the new birth, the bonding of my mind with the Holy Spirit (John 3:5-8) had taken place. I was a new creation! I would never be condemned in judgment (John 3:18); Jesus would change me (John 3:21). The rest of this work is a brief record of over fifty years of experiencing the phenomenal power of the Covenant Connection, over fifty years of miracles!

Later that summer Ray baptized me. The next week Libby and I were married. I was eighteen, and she likes to say she was almost eighteen. Few gave us much of a chance. With my track record, Libby would probably wake up one morning to find me gone. What folks didn't realize was that the miracle of the new birth had happened in me. Now that inner Power of the Creator was hard at work teaching me His way - and I cherished Libby. I had seen in her eyes, that, to her, my past was not significant. Even though I had absolutely nothing to offer her but my love, she had confidence in me. Libby trusted me, and knew, with God's help, I would become something. I would have died rather than betray that trust. Part of a song I once heard says, "You are the wind beneath my wings." Jesus has used Libby like that all the years we have been together.

As far as possible, I made restitution to those I had wronged. I was so thankful for a letter I received in return for one sent to the California Department of Transportation, detailing thefts I had taken part in. I had asked for an estimate of what I owed and requested time to finish school before repayment. The gentleman who replied said, "I perceive from your letter you have become a Christian. I, too, am a believer and rather than bring you to trial, I will pass sentence now. For the rest of your life you are to find youth who are struggling as you did and help them find the Way."

With God's help, I've tried to live up to his trust.

It's true Libby and I had no money, and I had yet to finish high school, but we had Jesus, each other, and a willingness to work. Easy? Certainly not. Money problems are the number one cause of the breakup of young couples, and we've surely had our share. We learned early on, however, that dependence on God to accomplish His will opens the way where there is no money. To watch God's providence in action like this builds a faith foundation that lasts a lifetime.

In the introduction I stated there would be examples given of prayer making the impossible, possible. Here's one. I finished two years at Southwestern Junior College convinced it was God's will that I get a four-year degree. Libby and I had been married four years; our daughter, Deborah, was two years old, and we were pregnant again. When Debby was born, Libby had been in labor for over seventy-five hours. Finally, our baby was delivered by cesarean section. I had been so afraid I would lose them both! Looking back, I can't imagine any doctor or hospital allowing a young mother to go through that. When I first held Debby, there were two stitches in her elbow caused by being nicked by the scalpel during the operation, as well as a small dent in her nose from being pressed against the obstruction in the birth canal. The enormity of the responsibility to protect that child at all cost became the dominant focus of my life at that moment. Libby and I agreed that our children, next to God, must be our highest priority. Debby was only a few months old when we decided that whatever happened, Libby must stay at home and care for her. If I couldn't earn enough to pay for school and support my family, I would quit school. We would not allow someone else to raise our children.

I was a broom-maker and being paid by the piece. This made it possible to more than quadruple minimum wage. I worked the summer after finishing at Southwestern to pay off my school bill and had 80 dollars left. We had chosen Southern Adventist University to continue my education. The choice had been simple: Southern had the best broom shop in the denomination, and I had called ahead for a job. Now, Fall enrollment was only a few days away and we were 1000 miles from Southern. Impossible? Certainly it was impossible, so we knelt on the floor and put our impossibility into God's hands. Then Libby and I loaded everything we owned: our daughter, her dog, and some food in our old Ford, climbed into that beaten-up old car and started for Southern Adventist University.

We arrived at Southern with 40 dollars left and began looking for a place to stay. As I mentioned earlier, this was a few days before school started, and there was no place available at any price, much less for the first month on credit. Night was rapidly approaching. What could we do? We did the only thing we knew to do, the thing that had consistently sustained us: we prayed. I returned to the university to check with the lady who was helping married couples find housing. As I entered her office, she looked up from her desk and exclaimed, "Oh, I'm so glad you're back. I just got a call from a couple who had put down a 35-dollar deposit on one of our furnished units. They are not going to be able to come to school. I asked if they would like for me to return their money. It was the strangest thing! They said, no, they had been impressed that there was someone who would need a place and might not have the money for the deposit. I was to let them have the apartment. Would you like to see it?"

I had no desire to look at the place first. I knew that what God had provided would be more than adequate for our needs. As the sun set, we moved in and thanked our Heavenly Father for a roof over our heads.

The next day I went to the College to apply and soon found myself looking at the business manager from across his desk. "Well, Mr. Stephens, we are happy you chose Southern. How much did you plan to pay for entrance?"

I had bought a few groceries and was down to 20 dollars. I replied, "I don't have any money."

There was a brief pause, and then, "Well, your folks are planning on helping you, right?"

I answered, "No, we'll be on our own."

Mr. Mann tried again, "Mr. Stephens, you have been in the service and will receive government benefits, correct?"

I again replied in the negative.

Mr. Mann was beginning to lose his smile, but he knew there had to be a logical reason for my being in his office. "I see you are married. Your wife intends to work to help pay for your education?"

I explained we had one child and another on the way, and my wife was going to stay home and raise our children.

Now, the business manager of Southern Adventist University was convinced this encounter was a waste of time for us both, and it was best to terminate an awkward situation as quickly as possible. Totally frustrated, he said, "Larry, there is no way you can attend this school!"

I looked the poor man straight in the eye and said, "Mr. Mann, I have a job at the broom shop. Give me a month and at the end of it, if I owe the school money, I will quit school, get a job elsewhere, and pay you back. However, at the end of the month, if you owe me money, I will come back to this office and collect."

This proposal was met with several seconds of silence as Mr. Mann sized me up. He said, "You're really serious about that, aren't you?"

I said, "Just give me a chance."

His reply, "You have a month."

At the end of the month, we had paid all our expenses, including my tuition, and the school owed me fifteen dollars. I returned to Mr. Mann's office to collect my money and request another month. This continued for the next three years until I graduated. Hard work? Yes, and I certainly wouldn't recommend what we did to anyone. For me, it meant working an average 35 hours a week during the school year and over 50 hours a week during the summer.

There was no vacation. On summer weekends, five buddies and I contracted with Purina-Ralston to catch chickens in their brooder houses. On average, these chicken houses contained over 10,000 chickens. For fourteen weeks the birds had never experienced darkness because the lights were never turned off. In this way, the chickens never roosted but were fed continuously, thereby reaching market weight rapidly. Before we arrived on Saturday night, those lights were turned off and, hopefully, the chickens would roost. If it was a full moon and a clear night, we knew we were in for a fight. Those conditions meant we would face birds fully conscious and ready to make us pay for their disturbance. The six of us would catch those 10,000 birds in between two and one half to three hours. This required running into the brooder house, catching seven chickens in each hand (14 chickens filled half a crate), running back to the truck to deposit our catch, and continuing this process until no chickens were left. Purina loved us. The company knew if a chicken house had contracted some disease and birds were near death, we could be counted on to get them loaded in time to reach a processing plant before daybreak. Industry regulations stipulated processing live birds only, but I can assure you we sent some horrible looking specimens to market that couldn't have lived another day.

I would arrive home at between two and three in the morning. Libby would meet me at the door and demand that I take my clothes off outside. You can never really appreciate the smell of a chicken house until you have run around in chicken litter dust for a few hours. It would usually be a couple of days before our olfactory nerves responded properly. A shower and tub bath to soak out the stench, a few hours of sleep, and I would be behind my broom winder at 8 o'clock on Sunday morning.

I have always been amused when anyone has suggested that Libby didn't work during those years. On those summer evenings, Libby and I would pick blackberries from the surrounding hills or glean green beans from harvested fields. These Libby would can in jars for use during the coming school year. Green beans and blackberries prepared in every imaginable way, along with Libby's homemade bread, constituted a considerable portion of our diet during those winter months. We purchased an ancient White treadle sewing machine with which Libby turned out clothes for herself and the children. Her expertise on that old machine earned many compliments for the neat appearance of my family.

Yes, it took a lot of hard work and sacrifice on the part of both Libby and me for me to receive a university degree, but hard work alone didn't account for making the impossible, possible. It was God's will that I finish school. By the way, I took a hundred-dollar-a-month cut in pay to go into teaching.

By God's grace, our marriage has lasted over fifty six years and is still holding! Libby is just as beautiful to me as when I was first smitten by her walk through the rice. Besides our two children, we have four grandchildren who are the lights of our lives! Many Sundays find us out on some lake fishing.

~ Chapter Two ~

Adventist Youth And The Covenant

The education phase of my ministry began in 1961 in Spartanburg, South Carolina, and continued 1964 through 1968 in Tallahassee, Florida. (I would receive my Master's degree from Florida State University.) In the fall of 1968, I arrived on the campus of Forest Lake Academy as the new Guidance Director. I had been under strong conviction for months there was a special work God would have done there, but I had no idea of the exact nature of the task. My first Sabbath morning on that campus, I told the students I believed God had a work for us to do. I wasn't sure what it was, but if any students wanted to search with me to find out, we would meet that afternoon at 3 o'clock. Forest Lake's reputation wasn't the best at that time, and I wondered if anyone would show up.

As the hour approached and no one came, I was getting ready to go home when the first students walked through the door; then more, until over forty had arrived. I was dumbfounded. Lord, here are the kids. Now what? That afternoon we talked of the need for Jesus in our school, the nearness of His return, and a world not yet warned of this event. Together, on our knees we began our search by asking God to please teach us what must be done to go home. The title chosen for that search was taken from 1 Corinthians 16: 22, "Maranatha," the Lord returns.

As we studied the Bible and the writings of Ellen White over the next few weeks, we came to the understanding that whatever we did must be focused on the Three Angels' Messages of Revelation, Chapter 14. We began working with local churches, usually on Sabbath afternoons. Our students would canvass the area door-to-door to find interests, then turn the names and addresses over to the church for follow-up. At the door we talked of Jesus, then read the Three Angels' Messages from the Bibles we carried with us. This was followed by these questions, " Have you ever had a chance to understand who Babylon is, or the beast, or the mark of the beast? Would you like to study the Bible to find out?" It was certainly an up-front, cold-turkey approach, but we were finding people who were concerned. It became increasingly apparent that a study guide was needed, designed to help people find the answers to our questions, one that would take a person step-by-step through the Three Angels' Messages. When I approached our local Adventist Book Center to inquire of such a guide, I was surprised to find none existed.

I had never done any significant writing in my life, but under the urgency of our situation an extremely rough study guide was turned out in two weeks. It was mimeographed and immediately put to use (Two years later, a much-refined version was printed by the Southern Publishing Association). As primitive as our materials and methods were, people were studying. Baptisms followed, and our students were beginning to realize a Power in our message they had no idea existed. Soon as many as fifty students a week were traveling all over the state of Florida with the message of Maranatha. At the time none of us knew what we had locked into. A spiritual explosion was about to take place on our campus.

One day Mike stopped by my office. Senior class president and an outstanding athlete, this, combined with blond good looks, made him a campus leader. Our conversation covered grades and college plans, but I sensed the real reason for this encounter was much deeper. Finally, I asked him, "Mike, why are you here?"

That boy looked at me a moment, and then asked, "Mr. Stephens, how can I know Jesus?" Taking a Bible we studied John 3:16.

After answering a few more of his questions, I had one of my own, "Mike, will you accept Christ as your Savior?" Mike and I knelt on the floor, and I listened to what has become to me the most exciting sound on earth, a sinner turning his life over to the SOUL HEALER! Mike left, only to return a few minutes later with four friends and a box filled with various types of alcoholic beverages. These young men had planned a party after lights out that evening, and the drink for the occasion had been hidden behind the recreation room refrigerator. Now these four joined Mike in commitment to Jesus. Within a week these five requested to meet with the student body in assembly with no faculty present. To say that meeting stunned those present is a vast understatement. Our students knew those boys as only students know each other and to hear them witness to the power of Christ ushered in a new awareness on campus. To have a vibrant, personal relationship with Jesus was no longer odd. Mike became Maranatha leader.

This turnaround had nothing to do with anyone's charisma or leadership. A revival can never be sustained in an Adventist setting that doesn't eventually focus on our responsibility to our message. We have been told if anything in our institutions is placed above the Three Angels' Messages, the gospel can't be the leading power. We may or may not believe this, my friend, but that makes absolutely no difference. God does. (Ample documentation for this, mainly from Scripture, comes later.)

The Spirit kept encouraging us to dig deeper, for the search must continue. As a result of a contact with young people of a different faith in St. Petersburg, we were invited to take a few students to Florida Bible College, a Baptist school, for a weekend. It was an opportunity for our young people to fellowship with those whose beliefs were different, and we were impressed to accept. From the time we arrived on that campus in Hollywood, Florida, on Thursday until we left early Sunday morning, we were involved in the most intense study of Scripture any of us had ever known. Not argumentatively, but in love, questions flew back and forth. It ended in absolute exhaustion at 3:30 a.m. on Sunday morning in a room filled with students and faculty from the College and our students studying the Three Angels' Messages.

On the way back to our campus the next morning the excitement of the past few days was causing an animated and lively discussion. The students in that car came to two conclusions: We needed a course in personal evangelism offered on the senior level, and they wanted to take a year out of school before starting college to learn soul winning. For my part, that intense study had revealed the close correlation between the third angel's message and the new covenant principles taught by Jesus and the apostles. I realized our message was God's last call to this planet to return to those principles. The Spirit was revealing connections between passages of Scripture I had never known existed.

That class in personal evangelism was started two weeks later with thirty seniors in attendance. Beyond classroom instruction, lab time tested what was learned. Bible studies were started which resulted in an amazing development; for the next two years young people who had never heard of Seventh-day Adventists before contact with our students would enter Forest Lake and enroll in personal evangelism. What a difference they made in classroom discussion! From that class of thirty seniors, eight elected to take a year off to learn to win souls. All eight were put with Pastor Tom Whitsett of Tallahassee, Florida. Yes, we had a lot to learn!

Over the next four years, as much time as possible outside of school duties or pastoring a church would be involved in the experiment we were beginning. Raising money; finding cars for transportation (I was always grateful for all those donated, but as you can imagine none came off a showroom floor, resulting in our kids learning auto mechanics); bicycles to use where possible; making sure room and board were adequate; checking out the pastors in charge of the districts involved; and prayer for guidance in uncharted waters were all involved. As far as money was concerned, a $1500 dollar scholarship was arranged between Southern Adventist University and the Florida Conference. Each student received a twenty-dollar-a-month stipend.

Before taking up duties in Tallahassee, our eight students, (four boys and four girls) spent a week at the Florida Conference youth camp, Kulaqua. Seminars were held on money management, auto upkeep, host relations, pastor relations, and obtaining and giving Bible studies.

Recreation was provided and was enjoyed, but all concerned were impressed with our need for soul searching and prayer, individually and collectively.

After Tom had everyone settled in Tallahassee, their work began. Working in pairs, usually boy and girl, they began following leads such as Voice of Prophecy respondents, former members, youth contacts made on their own or through someone else. Soon, small wooden racks were being placed in doctors' and dentists' offices and any other business that would allow it. In these racks were invitations to write in, requesting a free Bible along with a personal study program.

Tom was interested in what was called "dark county" evangelism, working in areas where very few, if any, Adventists lived. Our teams began directing an increasing amount of time toward Quincy, a small tobacco-oriented community west of Tallahassee. In order to help get started, a busload of Maranatha students from Forest Lake was sent to contact homes. Meetings were held for several weeks in a rented hall that ended with no visible results. All that work and apparently nothing to show for it was a real downer for our group. Tom led them in a day of fasting and prayer. For days there was a collective search in prayer for God's will.

Crawfordville

Crawfordville, Florida, is a small settlement close to the coast in the most sparsely settled and poorest county in

Florida, Wakulla. The county's only claim to fame is the world's largest spring named, aptly enough, Wakulla Springs. Work and, therefore, money are hard to find. Many residents work on the Gulf in the fishing or oystering business; others commute to Tallahassee or surrounding towns. Sandy driveways snake back into the woods to small dwellings, which more often than not, were mobile homes. One Adventist family lived in the county. The Lord said Crawfordville.

The only place that would accept a literature rack was, odd as it might seem, the post office. Responses to the invitations for Bible studies began coming in, and our teams started to work. In a few weeks, 86 of the 1100 inhabitants of the county were studying with our youth. Tom decided after a few months to try another series of evangelistic meetings and rented a shack in town called the Women's Club.

Flyers were prepared and distributed, advertising the meetings. Tom is an electronics wizard and one of the featured attractions was something he called "Talking Screens." In actuality, this involved two shower curtains on a frame, two slide projectors, and a tape recorder. Using rear projection, the slides were synchronized with the recorder in such a way that the images on the screen appeared to converse. For example, Jesus could speak with Peter. This might never have worked elsewhere, but it worked in Crawfordville!

As the meetings progressed, 25 non-Adventists steadily attended. At the end Tom made a call to accept Jesus and His

Three Angels' Messages. Having made only one other such public appeal, and that with dubious results, Tom waited for the response and was overcome with the thought that he had failed, - failed Jesus, failed the students, failed the audience, failed everybody. Overcome with emotion, he put his head in his hands and began to weep. He told me later he did part his fingers long enough to see a lady from Thailand who understood hardly any English get up and apparently start for the door. After a long pause, one of our students, Lynn Driver, tapped him on the shoulder and said, "Pastor Tom, you can look up now." Tom did as he was told and saw everyone in attendance that night surrounding him, many with tears. All had accepted his appeal, including the Thai lady. Later, when she understood the language better, Tom asked her how she knew to come forward. She answered that she had heard him in the Thai language and understood perfectly what to do! The gift of tongues?

Where could they meet? Certainly there was no money to buy or build a church and no place to rent. Tom made a hasty trip to Conference headquarters to see if a tent was available. An old cook tent was all he could find. Returning with the tent and a few folding chairs, he received permission to set up on a vacant lot. An old piano was donated and placed in the tent on wooden palettes to keep it off the dirt floor.

I must say that was the holiest tent I ever saw. When it rained, everyone received showers of blessings! I never heard that piano, but our workers told me most of the time it was soaking wet, and they were sure that sounds emanating from it had never come from wood and wire before! It was winter time, and Tom and some of his new members rigged up a heater made of stove pipe, heat strips, and a fan.

In a few weeks fifty-six persons were trying to crowd under the protection of that old canvas. Something had to be done. Another day of fasting and prayer was called for, and Tom and our students were joined by their new converts. Tom called the Conference to see if any help were available and was informed there was no provision to build churches in financially deprived areas other than the standard policy. This required most of the funds to be collected by a congregation before any Conference funds were used.

Tom prepared a special appeal for his people and traveled to Orlando, Florida, and our Conference headquarters to present it. As he was waiting outside a committee room before entering to present that appeal, the director of the Conference Association was passing by and stopped to ask why Tom was there. The Association is the legal arm of the Conference and is regularly bequeathed funds from estate settlements, often earmarked for a special purpose. Tom explained the problem in Crawfordville and was informed that there had been money set aside for such a project and a search was being conducted at that moment to find a suitable opportunity to use it. He was asked how much was needed.

Tom replied $25,000 would get them started. Together they left the Conference Office and went to a bank to draw out the necessary funds. Tom returned with a check for $25,000.

A nice piece of land was purchased in Crawfordville. An ingenious Tallahassee church member drew up plans based on plywood beams which could be easily assembled by hand. After those plans were approved by state engineers, our team members and their new Adventist friends began construction of the Crawfordville Maranatha Seventh-day Adventist Church. That little chapel made of local stone and wood is a monument to the faith of Adventist youth. If you are ever close to Crawfordville, Florida, some Sabbath, stop by and visit!

By the fall of 1973, things were really starting to move: Ten students were working in pairs in five areas of Florida; an Adventist church closed for the previous ten years was reopened in Homosassa, Florida; the Southern Union of Seventh-day Adventists had adopted Maranatha as its youth evangelism thrust; students at Southern Adventist University had established Maranatha leadership on campus and were sending the thrilling reports of God's guidance to us at Forest Lake; Maranatha studies on the Three Angels' Messages were being used in areas around the world; and a meeting with the General Conference of Seventh-day Adventist youth leadership resulted in establishing the Task Force Program of the church.

For me, personally, the greatest satisfaction came when our young workers returned periodically to Forest Lake to relate their experiences. For most of our students it was the first time they had ever witnessed the effect of the phenomenal power of the Third Angel's Message on the lives of their peers. There wouldn't be a sound in our auditorium. You could see the wheels turning in minds as those in their seats recognized the speakers as former classmates but no longer the same. The simple recitals of God's guidance carried fire right to the heart. That inner Power was transforming our campus. That time was so precious. It seemed we were so close to the fulfillment of Latter Rain promises. Even now, as I think back over the years, I see the eyes of so many Adventist youth burning in their love of the Master, in their determination to finish His work and in joy. I'll never forget the joy! May God grant us the grace to see in the eyes of many what we have seen in all too few.

Mike

I will always miss Mike Largin, the senior class president who did so much to help start Maranatha. As his last year at Forest Lake Academy ended, Mike planned to attend Southern Adventist University and enter theology. About the middle of his freshman year, I received word that Mike was in trouble; a little later I heard he was asked to leave Southern. I tried to reach him, but to no avail. Mike had entered the drug scene in Jacksonville, Florida, and had cut all ties with family and friends. I had to find him!

That summer I went to Jacksonville, located Mike's sister and asked her to help me find him. She said, "I will, Mr. Stephens, but I want to warn you, for us to find Mike we will be in places where both of us will be very uncomfortable. He's my brother and I'm willing to go, but do you really want to find Mike that badly?" I was more familiar with the element we would be entering than she could ever have known. I asked her, "When can we start?"

She hadn't exaggerated. In following the trail that led to Mike, we soon found ourselves on the Jacksonville waterfront among some very unsavory characters: pimps, whores, pushers, and dealers. The reactions from all of them to our questions were suspicion, fear, and antagonism. We couldn't convince them she was really Mike's sister, not a nark, and that I was a friend, not some brand of law. Finally, we were able to convince a drug dealer we were who we said we were and doing what we said we were doing. He told us he knew from our being in his area we were either the law or crazy. He had decided we were crazy and, since he had always had a soft spot in his heart for crazy people, he would tell us how to find Mike.

A rock concert was scheduled that night at the Jacksonville Coliseum, and Mike always sold drugs at a particular entrance. I was standing there an hour before the concert began. I certainly didn't fit in with the crowd there, and they let me know it: more suspicion, fear, antagonism. I could never take a lie detector test over the use of marijuana and pass after that night; too much was inhaled from the cloud of smoke around. The drug culture of that time was symbolized by leather, hair, and beads. Sure enough, I saw a figure walking toward me that resembled Mike in the way he carried himself but was all leather, hair and beads. He saw me but didn't flinch or walk away. When we were face to face, he said, "Hello, Mr. Stephens!"

I returned his greeting and after a few moments of conversation, I asked, "Mike, are you happy?" That question went right to the heart. The bravado was gone, and in its place his eyes showed that longing described earlier.

There was a long pause before he answered, "No, Mr. Stephens, I'm not happy." I told him when he was ready to be happy again, I wanted him to come see me. I had prayer with him and left.

Months went by, and I heard nothing from Mike. Then one day he appeared at my door on campus. The beads and leather were gone; he was in dress shirt and pants, clean shaven and a hair cut. After dinner with me, we went outside to talk. Mike wanted out of the drug scene but felt trapped. For one thing, he was in deep trouble with the law. I told him to turn himself in, face any consequences, and get on with life. Mike's eyes were so expressive. Now they were filled with sadness as he said, "Mr. Stephens, if I go to the police, I'll never live to see trial. The Jacksonville dealers won't allow it!" He further explained it wasn't so much death that concerned him. It was the way he would die that had him terrified. What can you do in situations like that but put it all in the hands of Jesus? I asked him what his plans were, and he told me he was leaving for South America that night. We had prayer together and he left.

More months passed. Then Mike was back at my door. The summer had just started. "Mr. Stephens, everything is cleaned up. I'll be working in Tampa this summer. Next fall I'm going back to Southern and take up theology again!" He never explained how all this had happened, and I never asked. My family and I just rejoiced with him through the evening, praising God.

A few weeks later, his sister called. The day before, Mike had been riding his motorcycle to work, was involved in a collision with a truck, and declared dead at the scene. I can't recall that moment without tears, and they are falling so fast as I type this that I can hardly see. So many times I have stood by the casket of a young friend, the scent of funeral flowers, the almost unbearable feeling of loss. At such times the universal question is, Why? We all know chasing that question is the ultimate exercise in futility.

Maybe Jesus knew this was the time Mike had to be taken for his own salvation, I don't know. I do know the more

I've found out about Mike's death over the years, the more I wonder how accidental it really was. Some time later, Mike's closest associate in the drug trade and his companions were machine gunned to death in Columbia, South America. I do know I will greet Mike again. I can hardly wait!

On my way home from school on a November evening in 1973, as I walked through a field, a Presence I can't even begin to explain stopped me in my tracks. I don't know how to describe the communication that followed. There was no voice, but the message was as clear as any conversation I've ever heard. The instruction: I was through at Forest Lake, and we were to sell our home immediately. There was no doubt The Holy Spirit was the Communicator. In confusion I replied, "But, Lord, things are going so well! How am I ever going to tell Libby?" There was no answer to that question (Friend, if what you're reading now seems weird, you should have been in my skin and lived it. The strangest part of this episode is still to come!). We had just finished our family room and, having done the work ourselves, were especially proud of the fireplace. The holidays were just ahead, and friends and family from chillier climes had made plans to visit. Sell our home?

Worship that evening with our two children was rather quiet. Afterward, when Libby and I were alone, I was trying to find appropriate words to break the news and bracing myself for the surety of being committed (I could see myself being chased by little men in long white coats determined to fit me in one of their tie-in-the-back sport jackets). But it was Libby who broke that silence. She turned to me and said, "Honey, I know you're going to think I'm crazy, but I've had the strongest impression today we must sell our home!" The house went on the market the next day, and we moved out the day after Christmas. In February we received a call to pastor the Pierre, South Dakota Seventh-day Adventist Church. We had never lived in the North before so we did a little research and found that both Florida and South Dakota have the same title, The Sunshine State. Well, that sounded nice enough! We were on the verge of learning about **COLD.**

Before leaving Florida, I returned to Crawfordville and the church that represented so much in the work of our young people. Alone on my knees in that small chapel, I asked God to allow me to live to see what had happened there with just a few students multiplied in the lives of many. I had witnessed in a small way what it would be like to finish our work on earth. I was certain that, through the Power of the Holy Spirit, the task could be accomplished. And that conviction lasts to this day!

The reason for the urgency demanded in selling our home didn't become apparent until a few weeks after closing. The bottom fell out of the Florida real estate market. If we had waited until the move to sell, we would have lost our shirts.

~ Chapter Three ~

Teaching

(As you will soon determine, I wrote this chapter before retiring from education.)

Recently, a group of my students gave me a plaque that reads:

A Hundred Years From Now

…it will not matter what my bank account was,

the sort of house I lived in or the kind of car I drove…

…but the world may be different because I was

important in the life of

A Student."

Come with me into my world, the classroom. Frustrating? Yes, occasionally. Stressful? Often. Challenging? Always. To me, it is intoxicating, exciting, and, ultimately, rewarding. What makes it so is relationships. In teaching, subject matter will always be important, but a teacher has a unique opportunity to impact the life of a child.

The trust that a student develops in these relationships will often last a lifetime and can be downright frightening. It was nearly midnight on a Friday evening that I received a call from a former student. She had a month-old baby out of wedlock and times were bad. Would Libby and I come, take her baby, and find a Christian home for it? That call originated from over 300 miles north of our home, but there was no hesitation in our response. We left early the next morning and, after spending a few hours with that young mother, we agreed with her that it was best to find a secure home for her small son. We left with the baby, a bottle of formula, a few diapers, and a note from the mother that read, "Larry and Libby Stephens have my permission (name) to find a home for (name)." That was it. There were no considerations for the legal implications of this. After arriving home, we immediately began checking with couples we knew who were looking for a child.

We could never be foster parents. That child was in our home for over three months and seeing him go was like giving up one of our own. As painful as that separation was, however, it didn't keep us from doing the same thing again a few years later!

It is true not every student will develop the level of trust described here. But in order to understand what it means over the years when they do, I want to tell about another Mike.

In 1964 we accepted a call to serve our school in Tallahassee, Florida. The school was located on ten acres of woodland, just outside of town. Students have a tendency to find out what a new teacher is made of and my 5th through 8th graders were no exception to this.

Shortly after school began, Mike led a delegation to my desk with a question, "Mr. Stephens, do you mind if we catch snakes and keep them in the room?"

I looked at this short little 5th grader and sized him up. This kid had moxie, and I liked him immediately. That first evaluation has stood for over forty years. I told him it was all right with me. Our school's location provided an excellent habitat for snakes. We all agreed, both boys and girls, to catch every non-poisonous snake on our ten acres. The next recess, we made capture sticks and started.

North Florida has several color phases of the rat snake. The white phase is known locally as a white oak snake and can grow to nearly six feet long. The markings on this beautiful reptile often cause it to be mistaken for a rattlesnake. We soon had about eight of them over five feet long, as well as black racers, Garter snakes, corn snakes, and other color phases of rat snakes. We also had a few specimens of the cute little hog-nosed snake that, when approached, will first spread a hood like a cobra and then, if that doesn't deter an attacker, roll over and play "possum." My students quickly learned which specimens would respond to their touch and which wouldn't.

Our prize exhibit, however, was Lucifer. One evening after school, Bobby, a 7th grader, was walking home when he saw a five-foot rattlesnake in a ditch. He promptly grabbed a stick, jumped into the ditch, and caught it. After getting it home, his father prepared a galvanized trashcan for viewing. First, he cut a large hole in the lid and riveted over it a piece of heavy metal mesh. The lid was then screwed securely onto the can. The next day, Bobby brought his catch to school. I can assure you, it really added a different dimension to "Show and Tell." The snake stayed coiled at the bottom of the can. If anyone stuck his or her head over that hole in the top, the big rattler would strike, mouth wide open, fangs extended, and invariably hit that metal mesh with a loud **SMACK!** There was no danger, but it didn't take long for my students to come up with an appropriate name: Lucifer.

One Friday afternoon we released all of our captives (except Lucifer!!) on the classroom floor to see how they would react to each other. Snakes were coiled in various places, and it seemed they segregated themselves by species. Some were probably no more than a foot in length while the larger rat snakes were close to six feet. There were at least fifteen animals on the floor. Just as our experiment was in high gear, the Florida Conference classroom supervisor stopped by for an unannounced visit. I was busy teaching in the front of the room when she walked in. One of my boys opened his desktop and a yellow rat snake he had tamed promptly came out. I glanced up to see she was having difficulty controlling her composure! Trying to get her mind off snakes, she noticed the garbage can in the corner and asked, "Oh, what do you have in the can?"

Before I could warn her, she walked quickly over and peeked in. The loud **SNAP** told me Lucifer had done his thing. I helped her to the couch in our small foyer. As color came back into her face, she looked up at me with an expression I'm sure one reserves for a space alien and then she quickly glanced at the front door. It was obvious she desired to terminate this visit as soon as possible and did so. I don't recall ever having another visit by a classroom supervisor. Probably, it was due to the fact that Tallahassee was so far from the conference office in Orlando.

In a few days we let all our snakes go so that they could hunt for food. Bobby donated his rattlesnake to a university for the benefit of science. Mike still talks to this day about the visit of our supervisor.

Our school was heavily involved with the annual Harvest Ingathering drive to solicit funds for the various humanitarian services of the Adventist church. From Thanksgiving to Christmas, my students worked to help meet the goal of their church. On many of those nights, Mike and I worked together in house-to-house solicitation. After the campaign, I always tried to do something special as a reward to the school for all the hard work. After the Christmas vacation of Mike's 8th grade year, I asked the students to suggest ideas for an appreciation activity. Mike held up his hand. I asked, "What do you have in mind, Mike?"

He was more than ready to answer, "Mr. Stephens, let's go on a canoe trip."

On the rivers in our area were numerous opportunities for a nice day-trip canoeing, and I was sure Mike had one of these in mind. I should have known better. "Where would you like to go, Mike?" I asked.

His reply, "Let's put in at Kulaqua and go to the Gulf."

Kulaqua is the Florida Conference youth camp located in the north central part of the state. I had no idea how far it was from that camp to the Gulf, but I knew we weren't talking "day trip." Both of Mike's parents worked for the state, so I told him to ask if they could find a map for the river system of the area. In a couple of days Mike brought his map, and we all gathered around to look. Starting at Kulaqua's spring that runs into the Santa Fe River; we would follow that river to the Suwannee River and then make our way to the small fishing village of Suwannee Town on the Gulf of Mexico; as nearly as I could tell, the trip would cover almost 100 hundred miles through some of the wildest wilderness in the state. After contacting the parents to get permission, I immediately assigned committees for the different aspects of the trip: one for food; another for procurement of canoes; yet another for camping supplies.

In March we gathered at Kulaqua: twelve students; our pastor, Elder David Manzano; a church member, Mr. Newlan (who knew something about canoeing); Libby and I, along with our two children, Deborah and Larry Jr. My daughter was twelve years old; my son, nine. We loaded our canoes with all the provisions we had planned for the trip and pushed off. Ahead of us lay four days of riotous adventure: of rope swings high over the water; of swimming in the crystal clear springs that feed the river system; and of observing the antics of the wildlife indigenous to the region. At night we pitched our tents under the stars and recalled together the day's activities around our campfire. On the last day we were eight miles from Suwannee Town when we were overtaken by a storm that whipped the water into three-foot whitecaps in a matter of seconds. The river at this point is over a third of a mile wide and absolutely devoid of any contact with civilization, other than a passing boat. There were no other boats in that storm. We found shelter when the wind was too strong and continued when it died down enough, always keeping the bows of those canoes pointed into the waves. It took eight hours to cover those eight miles, but there was never a complaint. As we approached Suwannee Town, the wind was at our backs and my indomitable crew rigged sails to carry them to shore, absolutely exhausted but exhilarated. Mike had had his canoe trip.

I continued taking that trip for twenty years with

from thirty to sixty Forest Lake Academy students. We called ourselves the Suwannee Swamp Rats, and those who went twice received a special trophy at a solemn induction ceremony before the student body. At this convocation they repeated together our Swamp Rat oath, "Against all obstacles, and any other precipitating circumstances, we will keep our T. P. (toilet paper) dry!" This was shouted as they held a roll over their hearts. I think you get the picture. It is true, that as I advanced into my sixties, the ground seemed to be getting harder and the trip longer. To give it up would mean I would miss being lulled to sleep at night by the sound of the river a few feet from my tent door; or being awakened by a raucous owl reunion in the trees overhead, as they hoot and yell, bragging to one another about their hunting prowess; or watching several flocks of white ibis fly into a crimson and gold sunset that takes your breath away, their black-tipped wings beating just above our heads; or hear the laughter of young people enjoying that which only the wilderness wonder can provide; to say hello, once again, to friends we have met along the river through the years. To lose all of this would leave a hole in my year that nothing else could fill, far too high a price! (I paid that price when I retired from Forest Lake Academy in 1999. I am 74 years old now. I still miss that trip!)

Our students were invited to go with us on camping trips and other excursions that might be of interest to them.

Mike was a regular. I had met a commercial fisherman, Kenny, with a 600-yard seine. I would occasionally go to the coast with him on Sundays to net fish. My main interest was just to see the variety of marine life that came up and, as you can imagine, usually several young people were with us. Kenny would dig a hole on the beach and place a pole in it with one end of the net tied to it. The rest of the net would be very carefully piled on a platform on the back of his skiff. Kenny would then row the boat in a semi-circle, letting the net out as he went. When he got back to shore, our job was to help him pull in the net. We had made a run through an area and had gathered nearly eight hundred pounds of mullet. Kenny decided to place the net in the same place again. This time, when we began pulling in the net, it seemed it was caught on some obstruction on the bottom. We were puzzled since there had been no problem before. Gradually, the net began to move. Our "obstruction" turned out to be two sharks nearly six feet long! Those who observed what took place next have argued ever since over whether these fish were sand tigers or bull sharks. At the sight of those fish, every bit of tomfoolery left in my system surfaced at once. I had always wanted to ride a shark, and this was the perfect opportunity. Kenny looked at me and asked, "What are we going to do with them?"

I was already pulling one of them back toward the water by its dorsal fin. Kenny immediately realized what was about to take place.

"You're crazy!" exclaimed Kenny. But he wasn't about to be outdone by a greenhorn like me. He began pulling the other one.

Once I got the shark in knee-deep water, I mounted the animal behind that dorsal fin, picked my feet off the bottom, kicked that shark in the tail, and held onto the fin in front of me for dear life! That fish shot out from shore like a rocket, as if it had been trained for such an eventuality from the time it was a pup. I looked back to see that Kenny had done the same thing and was no more than two or three feet behind. We were cutting through the waves in the general direction of Yucatan and our mounts were behaving beautifully. Pride goes before a fall, according to the old saying. All of a sudden, those powerful animals jerked their bodies in unison, and Kenny and I were no longer shark riding. Instead, we were treading water nearly 100 feet from shore. We were laughing together about this when I glanced out in the gulf and saw two dorsal fins begin to make a turn back toward us. Now, Jesus and Peter are the only two to ever walk on water, but I believe to this day Kenny and I should get honorable mention. I'm certain we broke all records getting out of the Gulf of Mexico.

I will never forget Mike's wide-eyed stare as I stepped on shore. My son and daughter thought they surely had lost their father and came running to give me a hug. Libby and

I had quite a discussion when we got home about the whole affair.

As reported earlier, I had accepted a call to Forest Lake Academy and moved to Apopka, Florida, the summer of 1968. Mike came as a dormitory freshman in the fall. I was allowed the privilege of watching that miraculous metamorphosis youth go through as Mike developed from a boy into a fine, Christian young man. There were the usual bumps along the way as he dealt with dating, breakups, and other problems associated with the teen years. After graduation, he was one of the eight Maranatha volunteers I sent to Tallahassee. Later, he trained as an emergency medical technician, and I began hearing about a fabulous young lady he had met. I stood with Mike and Patty at their wedding, and soon they both accepted jobs in Nome, Alaska. I can assure you, Mike was made for Alaska and vice versa. It didn't take long for him to assemble a dog sled team and, after several years of preparation, race in the Iditarod. For those uninformed, the Iditarod is a sled dog run from Anchorage to Nome, a distance of 1049 miles through some of the most beautiful and challenging terrain on earth.

Mike phoned one summer to announce the birth of their first child, a boy they named Verdry. He was beside himself with the joy and expectation of raising a son. Six months later, in the middle of the Alaskan winter, Mike called again. The day before had been 50 degrees below zero in

Nome. Mike and Patty had carefully wrapped their baby in preparation for the drive to church. When they arrived, they unwrapped a dead child. Crib death? We will never know. I can't even imagine the horror Mike must have experienced as he tried to use his training to revive his son. The funeral was to be held back in Florida, and Mike requested that I perform the service. Trying to help that young couple cope with that loss was one of the hardest things I've ever done. A day or two after the burial, Mike and I were together when he made the statement that let me know he would come through this experience spiritually intact. "Elder Stephens, just think, I'll be able to raise Verdry on streets of gold!"

"Yes, Mike," I replied. "You most certainly will!"

Mike and Patty now have two children, a boy and a girl. They know they are always welcome in our home and will stop by from time to time for a day or two when they are back in Florida. Mike's sled dog collection numbered 25 at last count and his daughter won the 2005 Junior Iditarod.

Relationships. I've taken a few pages to describe just a little about some. When our students leave us, it's as if we were standing on some lakeshore and skipping stones. Just as a rock will return to the surface again and again, so many of our young friends will make contact over the years, in person or by phone or letter. It may be to perform a marriage ceremony or just to attend one. It might be a request for a baby dedication or a baptism. More often than not, it's just a chance to touch base and catch up on the news, to get a handshake or a hug. Prayer could be needed as some difficulty is met. Believe me, phone calls can originate from any place on the planet and at any hour, day or night! On more than one occasion, these calls have come from jail or prison. Now, you see, as we stand on that imaginary lakeshore, it isn't just one or two stones on the water. Thousands are making their way into a glorious Son-Rise. That is the priceless treasure of teaching!

In my Bible Doctrines classes, the only book allowed is a Bible, and a special one at that. Each student's name is engraved in gold on an expensive, leather-bound, wide margin, New King James Version, capable of withstanding years of long, hard use. Those wide margins are used to keep notes as we chain reference our message through the year. That means the teacher in that classroom is not the human one. The Teacher becomes the Holy Spirit through the Word. Yes, we will use videos, invite guests in, have discussions on topics of interest, but the center of learning is that Bible.

This has created an amazing phenomenon: No matter where I travel, individuals who sat in my classes years ago will come up to me to express their appreciation for that Bible. They are using them to teach Sabbath school, or in the ministry, to bring others to a knowledge of truth. So many tell how they used that Book to bring a future mate into harmony with their beliefs. This has absolutely nothing to do with my ability as a teacher, but it highlights the fact we must train students to use the Word.

~ Chapter Four ~

The Plains

The pastoral phase of my ministry began in 1974 in Pierre, South Dakota. I look back on our time in Pierre with a sense of deep affection and awe: affection as I think of the wonderful friends we made; awe as I recall the power of His Covenant God displayed in such graphic examples.

The plains are engraved on my soul like no other place on earth. Generations of my family have lived and died on those wind-swept grasslands. The earliest connection by my family to this region I know of was an ancestor who died at a rundown, insignificant old mission called the Alamo. My grandmother's home was a simple shack on the prairies: a well, an outhouse, coal oil lamps, a garden. If any neighbors needed aid, they knew to find Granny, especially to care for the sick or dying. She was an excellent marksman with any weapon handy and carried a small 22 cal. pearl-handled revolver in her purse (mainly for rats). Tragedy had been so much a part of her life. Two sons died in a tornado, another in a gunfight (he was an excellent shot but just a little slow!). Willy, my youngest uncle, tangled with a rabid dog and died a horrible death. I knew I had an aunt, but no one ever spoke of her. I finally discovered she had killed her husband with an ax and was incarcerated. Only in the last few years did I find a picture of the couple; he was the meanest-looking man I had ever seen.

First, we must work on pronunciation. Pierre, South Dakota, is not pronounced "Pee-Air," it's "Peer" as in a fishing "pier." The South Dakota Conference contained 1,600 Seventh-day Adventists. I've never worked with more loving or concerned people in my life. My East Texas twang certainly stood out against their upper Midwest brogue, but my family and I were accepted wholeheartedly. Before I left Pierre, my parishioners were using the ultimate Southern idiom, "y'all." My district covered nearly 10,000 square miles and contained two churches and three Sioux Indian reservations.

As soon as possible, I wanted to start working with young people in South Dakota as we had in Florida. I placed a call to a young man who had already proven himself for over a year, Dennis Shafter. He was a Forest Lake Academy graduate and had been a theology major at Southern Adventist University. His studies were progressing well, and he had begun dating a fine young lady. In time, as the saying goes, he asked for her hand in marriage. A date was set, and soon announcements, arriving relatives and friends, decorations and flowers were all harbingers of the happy occasion. The night before the wedding, Dennis was called by his fiance' to be informed that the wedding was called off. Crushed? He was devastated. I asked him to work with us in Maranatha for the standard fifteen months. Then while working with the youth in our Winter Garden Church, he met another fine Christian young lady, and their relationship began to deepen. They had begun to talk about a possible engagement when Dennis received my call from South Dakota. It doesn't take much to understand the tangled emotions he tried to work through as he prayed for guidance. Finally, he sat down with Karen and explained he felt God needed him in South Dakota, and he would not be able to see her again for a year. An occasional phone call and letters would be their only communication. If, at the end of the year, she was still interested, their relationship would continue. I've never known a young person to make a more courageous decision. Dennis has mountains of faith and courage as will be documented shortly. (You want to find out what happened between Karen and Dennis, don't you? Well, you will just have to wait!) I called another Florida youth, Don, and received another affirmative answer. Two young ladies, Penny Nichols and Mitzi Inch, joined us. Later, Tom Whitsett was convinced he needed to accept a call to pastor the Sioux City Seventh-day Adventist Church. Students from Union College in Lincoln, Nebraska, were recruited to work with him. As needed, we called youth from both Florida and

Union College to continue youth evangelism in South Dakota. I saw the Holy Spirit do incredible things in South Dakota as the result of prayer; the following are just a few examples.

Charlie

Charlie is a South Dakota cowboy who lost his parents at an early age. One of our dear sisters had taken him under her wing as a special project for Jesus. He had inherited a home and small ranch, but many meals and much spiritual care came from Sister Diamond. She asked me to meet Charlie and, if possible, study the Bible with him. Charlie lived seventy miles away, but in my district that was just down the block. I called to make an appointment. Dennis had been located in that area and went with me.

Charlie quickly let us know his main interests were women and whiskey, not necessarily in that order. However, he did have some questions he would like to discuss. With his long hair, jeans, boots, and a deep tan, his words said one thing, but in his eyes I read a longing I was very familiar with. After a few visits spent answering his questions as best we could, we studied the gospel. I asked, "Charlie, will you accept Jesus Christ as your Savior?"

This was followed by a few minutes of silence, and then, "Mr. Stephens, I'm going to have to think about that."

Don and I had been working with interest in Pierre and were preparing for a baptismal service. Dennis was to continue studying with Charlie when possible.

Three days before the baptism, I was having prayer when that urgent impression that only comes from the Holy Spirit broke into my consciousness. I had to find Charlie today! That was no easy task. Charlie not only worked his own ranch but hired out to who knows whom or where in South Dakota or Nebraska. I phoned his home. No answer. I called Sister Diamond, "No, I haven't seen Charlie for several days, and I don't have any idea where he might be," she said.

Back on my knees, "Lord, if I must find Charlie today, You're going to have to lead me to him. You're the only one who knows where he is." I got into my car and drove out of Pierre toward the interstate. As I approached I-90, I prayed for guidance. Should I go left or right? I was impressed to go straight ahead. Soon I was on gravel; another road ahead, another request for direction. This continued for seventy or eighty miles as the crow flies; with all those turns I had no idea how far I had gone. I knew I was still in South Dakota; Nebraska is really good at putting their signs at the borders! I saw a curve ahead and was just going into it when I glanced to my left. About sixty feet from the fence bordering the road, Charlie was on a tractor coming my way. As he recognized me, I could see the surprise on his face. We met at the fence.

His first words were, "How in the world did you know where I was?"

Did I ever have a reply ready for that question!

"Charlie, the Lord told me you must make a decision about Jesus today and the Holy Spirit led me here to deliver the message!" I told him the time of the baptism on Sabbath, had prayer with him, and left. That Sabbath, as we were preparing to go into the water, there was no sign of Charlie. As you can imagine, his name had been mentioned repeatedly in prayer since I had left him. Then I heard the door behind me open, turned, and there he was! Long hair, western shirt, dress boots, as big a smile as you ever saw, holding a towel and his underwear! "I'm ready!" he said. And he was.

After we left Pierre, we weren't able to go back for several years. From time to time, through contacts with friends, we would get word of Charlie, maybe teaching a Sabbath School class or doing some other church activity. When we finally returned, Charlie was one of the first to greet us at the church door-- deep tan, long hair, western shirt, dress boots and that smile!

Betty

Pierre, although the capitol of South Dakota, is in actuality a typical Mid-western, small town with the emphasis on the western. Certainly the capitol buildings are there, but during our stay those buildings were no more than a quarter mile on the north side from the great American prairie that stretches for thousands of miles from Texas into central Canada. Thousands of head of buffalo are on ranches nearby as well as the multiplied thousands of cattle. In the summer the wind blowing on the countless acres of wheat causes waves to move across the fields, giving one the impression of being on a vast ocean of grain. Pierre is on the Missouri River and the world's largest earthen dam, the Oahu, is just outside the city limits. The reservoir it creates has made the town a center for fishing walleye, salmon, and trout.

A few hundred yards from the capitol is the most uniquely beautiful fountain created by an artesian well. Deep in the earth the well water mixes with natural gas. As the story goes, years ago a cowboy was passing by and noticed this water-gas mixture and wondered what would happen if he threw in a match. After the ensuing explosion, the ignited gas burned to a height of four feet off the top of the well. Later, South Dakota granite was used to build the fountain that exists today. The fire traces that gas deep into the well, then flows as fire and water mixed off the top of the well clear to the sides of the fountain. At night it is spectacular! So many times my family and I have enjoyed Friday night worship there. It always brought to mind the "sea of glass mingled with fire" of Revelation, chapter 15.

The water from the fountain is warm and flows into a small lake that never freezes. Thousands of Canada geese winter there each year. In the morning those geese spiral up from the lake in precise flight patterns to search for food on harvested fields. In the evening they return to spiral down in those exact same patterns. At a sunrise only the plains can create, in the deep cold, snow on the ground, hoar frost thick on the trees and sparkling pink in that early light, to watch those birds leave is one of the most majestic sights imaginable.

We were holding meetings in an old theater in town when we met Betty. From birth, she was without the use of her legs. In order to walk, she needed heavy leg braces and wrist crutches. Night after night she made her way to the auditorium to be with us. After a few days I found her address and paid her a visit.

As in most small Mid-west towns, the buildings are two-story brick. Above the shops on the lower floor are businesses interspersed with small apartments. Betty lived in one of those tiny two-room apartments on the second floor. To go to work, she walked about eighty feet down a hall to a telephone answering service on the same level. In order to reach her living/work quarters from the street, she had to maneuver those crutches and braces up one flight of stairs to a small landing and then go another flight to the second floor. I have no idea how that child got groceries or other supplies up those stairs. Betty's world mainly consisted of making her way back and forth between work and her apartment.

After the presentation of the Sabbath, Betty requested a visit. We sat around her kitchen table as Scripture was referred to in answer to her questions. When it seemed she had been satisfied, I asked, "Betty, how do you feel about the Sabbath?" Her reply was so simple, "Pastor Stephens, I want to keep the Sabbath." She didn't think arranging work would be a problem; it hadn't before when she had needed a Saturday off. She asked if I could come by to take her to church next Sabbath and was told, certainly. Our little church went out of their way to make Betty feel at home. After the service we enjoyed a good Sabbath dinner together and later that evening, we took Betty home.

On the following Monday Betty explained to her employer her need to be off on Saturdays. After learning the reason for this request, her employer launched into an angry tirade about cults that practiced mind control and caused innocent victims to make stupid requests like Saturdays off! If Betty didn't show up for work the next Saturday, she was fired! In response to Betty's call, I returned to her apartment. It doesn't take any effort to understand the dilemma she was in; it was her world or the Sabbath. In our discussion it was emphasized that Jesus always stands with us in trial and honors our decisions to follow His example. I asked if she wanted me to come by for her next Sabbath and received an immediate, "Yes."

After a second Sabbath with us, we again returned to her apartment that evening. I stood at the bottom of the stairs as she began that laborious climb. I could see at the top of the second flight a woman was standing, hands on hips, watching

Betty's progress. Just before the landing at the end of the first stairs, her employer screamed, "You're fired, Betty, and don't ever bother to ask. You'll never work for me again!" Betty returned home with me.

Our message cuts so deep! I've seen it rip families apart, alienate friends, separate husband and wife, cause loss of employment! Observing this kind of trauma tempts you to blame yourself. Are you sure what you're preaching is important enough to cause this kind of hurt? My brothers and sisters, our only response is to turn to Jesus. On our knees with those who are suffering so severely, we search for the Master's solution.

We began calling to see if there were a state agency that dealt with the problems of the handicapped. We were successful and after making an appointment, I took Betty for an interview. She was informed the state offered job training along with a small stipend to help with expenses until work was acquired. The stipend would be enough to cover her present expenses, and the church helped until the program began.

Betty requested baptism. I was concerned over getting her into our small baptistry and suggested waiting until summer when we could use the river. Betty is a determined young woman and didn't want to wait. I had a Baptist friend in town who had attended one of our Stop Smoking seminars. After a thirty-five year, two-pack-a-day, tobacco habit, he quit and together we praised God for his deliverance. I asked him how he would care for a situation like Betty's in his church. He replied, "Larry, we had a person in that condition once. We placed him in a metal chair, put two deacons in front and two in back, carried him into the baptistery and baptized him, chair and all!" That's how we baptized Betty.

A few months later, Betty's training required a move to Rapid City. Before she left, we enjoyed a last worship together by that lake and fountain described earlier. Shortly after that we received a call to return to Forest Lake Academy. Some years passed and friends from South Dakota stopped by to visit for a few days. During our conversation, Betty's name was mentioned, and I asked if anyone was in touch with her. The reply, "Yes, and she has a baby!" brought me out of my chair.

My response, "How did that ever happen?" (I realized how stupid that question was as soon as it left my mouth. Oh, well!) About a year after Betty's arrival in Rapid City, evangelistic meetings were being held. Betty had volunteered to help. A young man she assisted in Bible study was able to see beyond the braces and crutches to Betty's real beauty. He was baptized, and they were married. My mind returned to Betty's world when I had first met her: those two tiny rooms, and that dingy eighty-foot walk to work. I recalled the struggle of spirit she had gone through in deciding between that world and the faith walk with Jesus. The Lord had given her a new world, one that contained a husband, a home, and a child to raise! Yep, funny how things work out!

Roger

The Mormon organization is strong everywhere, but especially in the West. Our young missionaries were meeting their missionaries, and from time to time we would have them all, theirs and ours, over for lunch or dinner. It's hard for Mormon youth to relax in the home of someone of a different faith, but as time passed, friendships deepened.

Roger was a staff sergeant and the army recruiter for our part of South Dakota. Heavily decorated for his tours in Vietnam, he was a very tall, muscular, and imposing individual. He and his wife were contacted by one of our teams and became interested in studying with us. As their interest grew, they began coming to church with their three children. Late one night, Roger called to ask if I could come over. When I arrived at his home and was invited in, I was surprised to find not only Roger but those two young Mormon missionaries we knew so well. Roger placed me at his kitchen table opposite those boys and explained, "Brother Stephens, we've been studying with you Adventists and these Mormon boys as well. We're going to decide tonight whether to become Mormons or Adventists. I want you and these boys to study about the Sabbath using your Bibles. I'm going to sit in my chair over here and listen. When I've decided which one of you is right, I'll let you know!" With that, he placed his huge frame in an equally huge, black swivel rocker, faced the wall with his back to us, and slowly began to rock. I quickly sent up a silent petition for the Spirit of Truth to be present in the name of Jesus, and then asked those boys to pray before we began. I felt a little sorry for those kids since being restricted to Scripture made them like ducks out of water. After about thirty minutes, Roger turned that big rocker around to face us. We stopped in our tracks. Walking over to the two young Mormons, he said, "Thank you, gentlemen, I appreciate your taking the time to be here. Good night." With that, he ushered them to the door. Two weeks later, all five of his family joined the remnant!

Having read the hurt and dismay on the faces of those Mormon boys, I wanted a chance to visit them. A couple of days later I found their address and drove over. Only one was home. The atmosphere was chilly, to say the least. After some small talk and a short discussion on Biblical validity, I made a proposal. Having learned there is little, if any, hope of influencing members of the Mormon faith as long as their hold on Joseph Smith can't be broken, I asked, " You have a prophet that you believe with all your heart had a message from God, right?"

A rapid and heartfelt, "Yes!" was returned. I said, "I have a prophet I believe with all my heart had a message from God. The problem is, their messages don't agree. One of those prophets is lying! Tell you what! Let's kneel together and ask the Holy Spirit in the name of Jesus to reveal to us right here and now which prophet is true."

I have seldom, if ever, seen the horror expressed on the features of a human as I witnessed on that young face as my proposition struck home. I had become the Devil! Rather than accept the offer, or even speak, the boy backed out the door of his apartment as he held those horrified eyes on me, turned, and walked down the street. I never saw him in Pierre again.

The second church in my district was eighty miles from Pierre in White River, South Dakota. A few miles away was the Rosebud Indian Reservation and just outside of town a small grouping of government-built Indian homes was under reservation jurisdiction. Soon after Dennis arrived, we made our first contact with the Sioux. I had become well acquainted with poverty in Haiti while helping establish medical clinics across the country, but this was different. It was the hopelessness of a disenfranchised people. Alcohol, spirit worship, and that hopelessness make a volatile mixture, and we had entered a different world where the Spirit of Jesus would be in direct confrontation with the spirits of Satan.

We were getting ready to hold meetings in White River and were going door-to-door, becoming acquainted with the people and handing out brochures inviting them to attend. After canvassing the town, we began contacting those Indian homes nearby. No one was home at the last house we called on, so we left a brochure and walked away. We had no way of knowing the drama that would be played out in that small dwelling for the glory of God.

Our meetings were held in the local American Legion Hall next to the town liquor store. This close proximity developed into some uniquely interesting evangelism! Many of those in attendance were choosing to get a healthy supply of alcohol next door, and then would come to us for a hefty dose of religion! One Saturday evening a large tribal member stood in the back while I was preaching and began speaking loudly in a language I had never heard. I noticed he was copying my every gesture and body movement. No one seemed to be bothered, and he was much larger than I, so I let him alone. Later I found out he had been translating every word into the Lakota or Sioux language and had been trying his best to get those gestures right. The next week he returned for a repeat performance, but midway through, passed out, fell to the floor, and began to snore. After the service I went to him to help him outside before we locked up for the night. From his back pocket I took a bottle of liquid called Ever Clear, one hundred and ninety proof, ninety-five percent straight alcohol. I was to discover this was the preferred hard liquor on the reservation. If there ever was a Devil's brew, Ever Clear certainly qualifies.

Sam

A young couple, Sam and Pansy, became regular faces in our nightly group. Dennis and I found their address and stopped by to visit; it was that last house on the street where no one had been home before. Sam wasn't home, but Pansy didn't mind if we came in for a few minutes. As we talked, Pansy became more at ease and finally told us Sam had a problem, alcohol.

I made it a point to return when Sam was home. In the course of our conversation I learned Sam was Choctaw, originally from Oklahoma, while Pansy was Sioux and a South Dakota native. I never determined how those two ever got together with homes so far apart, but for Sam to live on a Sioux reservation was a constant source of irritation. The Sioux are suspicious of anyone outside the tribe and especially an Indian from another tribe. For example, Major General Armstrong Custer had used Crow scouts as guides through Lakota territory, including their sacred Black Hills. This was as hotly discussed among the Sioux in the 1970's as if had happened the previous week. When I was in South Dakota, no member of the Crow tribe dared set foot on a Sioux reservation for fear of his life.

Many Sioux seemed to go out of their way to pick a fight with Sam. It would seem that after a while, they would have learned better. Sam was a powerfully built young man with a well-deserved reputation as a fighter. With no more than two or three Sioux opponents, he hardly worked up a sweat! As my soul bonded with his, I became increasingly aware of his almost casual attitude to the brutality and violence surrounding him.

Sam would not let me become involved in that danger if he could help it. I was with him behind his house when a shot rang out, followed by a scream. I started for the front to see if I could be of assistance when Sam grabbed me, pinning me to the side of his home. Looking me straight in the eye, he said, "Brother Stephens, you didn't hear anything and you're not going to the street to see anything either!" A bridge crossing the White River was less than a half mile away. A day or two later the body of a gunshot victim was discovered under that bridge. I'll never know if his anguished last cry was what I heard.

Wounded Knee is on the Rosebud Reservation. The uprising there of militant Indians that resulted in a standoff with government authorities had happened the year before. A strong residue of hatred and resentment still existed among the Sioux. Sam and I were talking in a park and unaware of a meeting of the militants in our area taking place nearby. When it was discovered that a white man was close, we suddenly found ourselves surrounded. It not only became evident I wasn't welcome in the vicinity, but the looks on the faces around me said this situation could get really nasty. Just recently a young pastor of a different faith had been killed on Rosebud. Sam quickly went to the leader of this group and pulled him aside. Again, I'll never know what was said, but the result was an announcement in Lakota to the crowd that calmed everyone down.

For months Sam would be a hard-working, devoted father and husband, and then a transformation would take place. Becoming restless and ill at ease, his eyes would show a longing nothing could satisfy but alcohol. For the next two to three weeks, Sam and his friends would rampage over northern Nebraska and South Dakota drinking, fighting, and running from the law. To meet Sam drunk was to face the unleashed power of a demon. Pansy's body bore the scars of beatings received from her husband, and their two children lived in constant fear of their father in that condition. At such times Sam's family would do their best to hide from him with relatives or friends until he sobered.

When the binge was over, their home would look as if it had been in a war zone: the floors and beds were covered by an odious mixture of mud, liquor, urine, and feces; clothes, dishes, pots and pans were scattered; broken windows were framed by torn curtains; everything of any value was sold or hocked to buy alcohol. Sam would be so ill with alcohol sickness he could hardly move; a white, gummy substance coated his mouth and lips. Don was another of my Forest Lake students that had come to join us in South, Dakota.

Dennis, Don, and I would help Pansy clean up the mess. On one such occasion Sam called me over to the couch he was lying on, took the lapels of my coat in his big hands, and with longing in his eyes I can't describe, pleaded, "Brother Stephens, please help me get over this!"

Not only did I feel helpless, but my own faith was being severely tested, "Lord, can this man overcome this? I believe, but please help my unbelief!"

Pansy's birthday was near, and Sam had been drunk for a week. No one knew where he was, although reports had come in from several police departments about his activities. Wanting to cheer the family, Don and Dennis had planned a simple birthday party for Pansy. Sam's family was staying with Pansy's parents in a two-room shack. Pansy's father was not only well respected among the Sioux but in the town of White River as well. Just a month previous to this, his family had lived in a fine, two-story home. One of Pansy's older brothers returned from a bar at about two a.m. one morning and thought he saw a spirit in the house. He returned to his truck, got a five-gallon can of gasoline, poured it all around the foundation of the home, threw in a match and drove away. Miraculously, the family escaped unharmed, but with only the clothes on their backs. Now the father, mother, two brothers, a sister, Pansy, and her two small children were trying to exist in those two rooms next to the burned-out remains of that house. Don, Dennis, and I had been collecting clothes and other necessities for them and had delivered several items, along with a birthday cake the boys had prepared for Pansy.

The party was going on in one of those small rooms, and I was in the other with Pansy's parents when the door crashed open. There stood Sam. He saw the cake on the table with candles lit and Pansy with Don and Dennis. Sam was not only under the control of alcohol but a spirit as well who told him my workers were there to seduce his wife. Sam shoved Dennis aside, yanked up Don and pinned him in the corner. As I entered the room, one of those big hands had Don by the throat; the other balled into a fist and cocked. There would be no time to tap Sam on the shoulder and suggest we talk it out. It was very evident Don didn't have that kind of time. I grabbed Sam, turned him around, and pushed him back against what was left of the front door. We were a little over a foot apart. Those eyes with all that hatred focused on my face, and it seemed I was looking right into the soul of Satan. This was a man who had not only saved me from harm but with whom I had spent hours in study and prayer.

From time to time before a particularly dangerous stunt a program announcer will give the disclaimer to never try this at home. What I will relate had nothing to do with a stunt. I was determined to give the Holy Spirit a chance to use the soul bond between Sam and me to reach Sam.

I said, "Sam, if you're going to hurt anyone here tonight, you'll start with me. If you're going to beat up anybody here tonight, you'll start with me. You want to kill someone here tonight, Sam?" The knife used to cut the cake was on the table. I offered it to him and said, "Take it!"

I watched the power of the Holy Spirit penetrate even that drunken mind. The hatred began to leave those eyes. He hung his head and said, "I can't do it!" We stayed with him most of the rest of that night as he sobered up. In a few weeks I baptized Sam.

A few days after Sam's baptism, I received the type of call that can devastate a pastor. After being repeatedly turned down for work, Sam had returned home utterly discouraged. Friends had stopped by and Sam had left with them and a bottle. Now Pansy was calling me for help. The prospect of facing Sam drunk again sent a chill through me, but I knew I had to go. People may have warned me about working with drunk Indians, but I couldn't let that soul bond with him be broken. I covered the eighty miles to White River as rapidly as possible, praying Sam could be found before alcohol was dominate.

On arrival, I found Pansy and the children had already gone into hiding, just as they should have. After searching the town for his car with no success, I began with the bars. He was in one with those friends when I approached his table. I said, "Excuse me, but Sam is needed at home." Taking him by the arm, I led him out of the bar and into my car. There have been two times in my life I spent praying through the night for someone's soul; this was to be one of them. I called Libby to tell her I wouldn't be home until, hopefully, the next day. I gave her no reason; she was to know little of what was happening on the Reservation until after we left South Dakota. I put Sam to bed and knelt beside him. When he was awake that night I prayed with him, while asleep I prayed for him. The words I used I no longer remember; I recall desperation; I had a desperate hold on God that in some way this man would be released from the hell that bound him. And fear. Fear for myself? You bet! Far more than that, however, I was afraid for Pansy and those children. They had already suffered so much. The sun finally came up and Sam awoke. Praise God, as he turned toward me, I could see his eyes were clear!

He looked at me and asked, "You've been here all night?" I told him yes, and then he said, "Well, you can go home now. I don't want any more to drink."

Sam's battle with the bottle wasn't over yet, but God did finally deliver him from the hell of alcoholism. Sam and his family moved off the Reservation and we lost contact. Fourteen years after we left South Dakota, the phone rang late one night. That certainly wasn't unusual, but when I picked up the receiver the voice on the other end said, "Hello." Okay, so what's so unusual about that! There are some voices you recognize when just the first syllable is heard. For me, this was one of those.

I said, "Sam, where are you!"

He explained he was back in South Dakota working for the government and had been trying to locate me all those years. After spending a few minutes catching up on the news of our families he said, "Brother Stephens, I just wanted you to know I'm still dry and I'm still with Jesus!" Isn't it amazing how God works some things out?

Pansy

I don't know that I ever met a Sioux shaman or medicine man. From what I was told on the reservation about their abilities, authority, and power, I would put them up against any witch doctor on the planet! Many on the reservation were accustomed to seeking advice and healing from a shaman. As explained to me, when the shaman was consulted, he would go into a trance in order to confer with the spirits. After receiving an answer to the problem or power to heal, whatever was needed, he became the medium through which the spirit's blessing was bestowed. When I began working on the reservation, many Indians wanted to know what my Jesus could do in comparison to a god named, say, Uweepee (I told you I never did learn how to pronounce those names, much less spell them!).

One day a mother brought a sick child for me to heal. I don't recall there was anything so seriously wrong, and free medical assistance was available on the reservation, but this mother wanted me to pray for her baby. I happened to have a small bottle of olive oil in my car which I retrieved. After explaining the Christian's admonition on healing in the fifth chapter of James, I anointed the baby and asked for him to be healed in the name of Jesus if it was God's will. She left and I never saw her again to ask how her child fared. Evidently he fared pretty well. Soon, every time I reached Rosebud, requests would be made to anoint the sick. That little bottle of oil opened many homes. That Jesus power in comparison with other gods was doing very well, thank you!

One day I received a call from Pansy requesting a visit. She was pregnant and close to delivery, but had a problem she couldn't solve. Pansy and Sam had a fourteen-month-old baby with extremely severe spina bifida. There had never been one sign of recognition or any other form of intelligence displayed by this child. The baby required constant care; hence, the problem. Pansy told me, "Brother Stephens, I'm going to have a new baby soon, but Little One takes all my time. How am I going to care for both babies?"

I knew there were institutions on the reservation to care for children like Little One and told Pansy so. I should have known better. Sioux tribal tradition will not accept such a solution. She answered, "No, Brother Stephens, I can't place my baby with strangers!" I asked, "Pansy, are you willing to let Jesus find a solution for your problem?" After thinking it over for a moment, she said yes. We knelt together and both of us placed Little One in the hands of Jesus. This was on a Thursday; on Monday another call came from Pansy, this time from the reservation hospital. Little One had been a healthy child other than her birth defect but that morning she had suddenly become seriously ill. Her parents requested I be with them. By the time I covered the one hundred and ten miles to that hospital the child had died. Sioux tradition calls for a wake before burial so we scheduled the funeral for Wednesday.

That Wednesday dawned very cold and snowy. I arrived at the small chapel chosen for the service to find Sam but no Pansy. Sam explained that Pansy had gone into labor that morning and was in the hospital giving birth. We buried the one child, then rushed to the hospital in time for the arrival of their new daughter! A few days later I dropped by to see how mother and baby were doing. As Pansy held her infant, I asked if she thought Jesus had answered her prayer. She looked up at me, smiled, and said, "He answered it the only way it could have been answered."

That's Jesus for you!

The V.W.

My little Volkswagon Super Beetle was purchased in Florida but was well suited for South Dakota. With the weight of the motor on the rear tires, traction in the snow was exceptional. As demanded by my parishioners who seemed to be convinced my inexperience with South Dakota winters was destined to cause my demise, I kept the standard shovel, large candle, sleeping bag, tire chains, and extra food in the front cargo compartment at all times. Other than those chains, I never needed the other stuff, but several times thought I would and was thankful it was there. Many times between leaving Pierre to make a call some place on the prairie and returning home, blizzard conditions would develop. As that little car busted drift after drift of blown snow, I would pray it didn't stop! My only gripe was the heater which was evidently engineered to keep a person just out of deep freeze. This also meant the windshield defroster did an excellent job in the South Dakota hundred degree plus summers, but too often I would arrive home peering through the bottom two or three inches of glass in the winter.

The "beetle" did serve as an ambulance, if required. For instance, Don and I were returning to Pierre after midnight and going into a sharp curve when we saw a truck overturned some distance from the road. It looked like the accident had happened some time ago and, being very tired, we had no interest in stopping to investigate. I was ready to floor it when something warned me, stop! The truck was lying on its passenger side with all the glass broken out. We climbed on top and looked in. Staring back at us were two eyes in what seemed to be nothing but blood. When we got the man out, he was covered in so much blood and had so many holes in him, I had no idea how to stop the hemorrhage. We helped him to the V.W. and leaned him against the side while Don got in the back behind the front passenger seat; then I helped him into that passenger seat. I told Don whatever happened, not to let him go to sleep. We made the seventeen miles to town as fast as the little car would go. After leaving him at the hospital emergency room, Don and I went home. Before going into the house, I took a hose and rag and washed blood from all over the inside of the car. The outside looked as if I had driven it through a slaughterhouse, so that was washed as well. Believe it or not, for the next couple of weeks, every time I washed that car blood ran from under the trim. I still don't see how anyone could lose that much blood and live, but he did!

Another emergency called me back to Rosebud. It was very cold, probably ten or fifteen below, but I hadn't seen ice on the road. My speed was close to seventy-five miles an hour as I topped a hill and hit ice. As far as I could see, the highway was glazed with it. Much more quickly than it takes you to read this, that car had turned one hundred and eighty degrees, and now my back glass was my windshield. The speed on that glare ice was still seventy-five miles an hour! I had never realized telephone poles whizzed by so rapidly at that speed. I put my arm on the passenger seat and turned to look through my used-to-be-back-glass-now windshield. By this time the little car had drifted over into the oncoming lane, and I decided the first thing I saw coming my way would probably be the last thing I saw, period. I have been told there is no reason to get upset over things you can't control, and the V.W. was definitely out of control. A really good time for prayer!

"Lord, I know I was speeding and You know how much I regret that right now. However, those folks in Rosebud really need my help, and I can only see three ways this can end: me in the hospital, or dead, or You're going to have to do something with this car. **Please!**"

I promise to relate exactly what happened, and to the best of my ability I will not add to or detract from. I was still going downhill at about the same speed I had hit the ice. That car turned back around and began to slow down and continued slowing until it went off the road into some ice-covered grass. Once it reached fifteen miles an hour, I put it in gear and went on my very thankful way. From time to time over the years since then, the Lord has used officers in various types of uniforms to remind me to obey speed laws.

Those Maranatha workers, by the way, have gone on to serve God, church and country in so many ways. Dennis did return to Florida, and he and Karen were married. (You knew it would have a happy ending, didn't you?) He and Karen have two children and Dennis is a conference official.

~ Chapter Five ~

God's Call

When I finished Chapter 4, I certainly had no intention of ever leaving teaching. As you have probably noticed, I had become complacent in a vocation I thoroughly enjoyed. It just doesn't seem that our Lord has much respect for complacency.

My daughter Debby, her husband, Brent and their three children had moved from Florida to Hinsdale, Illinois. Brent was a vice president of Hinsdale Adventist Hospital. We had gone from almost daily contact to communication by e-mail, telephone, or letter. We missed them so.

For years my main hobby had been rebuilding old Chevrolet convertibles. I had finished and sold two Impalas, a 1961 and 1964. For you car buffs, the '61 was powered by a 348-cubic inch V8 with a three-speed manual transmission with overdrive and shift on the floor. The '64 was triple black with a hopped-up 283, with 4 on the floor. These cars had been driven all over the country before being sold and had provided so much enjoyment for Libby and me. We loved to hear their deep-throated dual exhaust.

While rummaging through a junkyard in Louisiana, I found a 1961 Chevy convertible I had never seen or heard of. Its trim was so unique. After returning to Florida, a little research revealed the car was a 1961 Chevy Super Sport. Late in the 1961 model year, General Motors wanted to introduce the Super Sport concept. To do so, four hundred and sixty-four Impalas were pulled off the line, the new 409-cubic inch motor was installed; special brakes, suspension, and trim were provided. No one is sure how many convertibles were built, but the estimate is no more than fifty. That old car was so rare! I returned to Louisiana, purchased the Super Sport, and brought it home. It was in terrible shape, but I could envision it looking like new: white body with a red stripe, a red and silver interior, and duals behind that huge 409 with 4 on the floor.

Brent, my son-in-law, had an intense love for auto mechanics and had experience rebuilding old Chevys. He was the fastest man with tools I have ever worked with, and we began working on the Sport immediately. Soon we were joyously up to our eyebrows in grease and dirt. We traveled extensively searching for those rare missing parts. When Brent took the call to go to Illinois, I was so happy for him, but losing him seemed to take the wind out of my sails. Working on the old car wasn't the same.

When the 1999 school year began at Forest Lake Academy, I realized a change I had never expected. The thrill and anticipation weren't the same. They weren't gone entirely, but I recognized the symptoms. God was calling me to something else, and at first I faced this realization with shock and obvious questions: What? Where? When? Was I experiencing burn out? Long ago I had determined if I ever began the journey down this particular slippery slope, I would get out. But I knew burn out wasn't involved. God had a different plan. Early in October I went to my principal and told him this was my last year. I knew I had to get out, and it wasn't fair to the school to delay the search for a replacement. Now it was his turn to be shocked. Was I sure? What are you going to do? Where are you going? Are you sure God is talking to you? I had no answer to any of these but the last one. Yes, I was sure God was talking to me.

The family room in our home had an outside wall that was thirty-two feet of glass, eight feet tall, and allowed us to observe birds, animals, and kids in our back yard. I had built a tree house with catwalks to surrounding trees. Libby's flower gardens were known to her family and friends as her "nursery." Orchids and bromeliads grew under the live oaks in the corner. We were so happy, so complacent. Surely God's plans, whatever they were, wouldn't involve leaving our home. Surely not.

As we prayed through this time of uncertainty, I

began to be drawn to hospital chaplaincy. Our Adventist hospitals were located in several close communities. Maybe this was God's plan. I discovered several units of Clinical Pastoral Education were required to enter the field and made application to receive this training at Florida Hospital.

In November, our daughter Debby informed me that the search was on for another chaplain at Hinsdale Adventist Hospital. I made inquiry about this with the Director of Ministry, Jonathan Leach. Jonathan told me he was coming to Orlando, Florida, for meetings and would like to meet for lunch. During this time we exchanged questions, backgrounds, and common acquaintances (those Adventist connections!) When Spring break came at Forest Lake, Libby and I flew to Chicago to visit Brent, Debby, and the kids. I took some time to visit Hinsdale Hospital, met with Jonathan's manager for chaplains, and left a resume. The next day he called to ask if I would take a day to interview with several department heads. I replied in the affirmative and did so.

I knew there was little, if any, chance of receiving the position. I was familiar with some of the other applicants and realized their experience and training in the field would far outshine a novice like me. You can imagine my surprise when I received a call from Jonathan offering me the position. He informed me I would be trained at the hospital, and arrangements would be made for Clinical Pastoral Education.

If I accepted, it meant leaving our home. Libby had

no interest whatsoever in leaving Florida, even if it did mean being close to Debby and Brent. She has never been at a loss for words to state her position, and this occasion certainly was no exception! I could go to Illinois, stay in an apartment, and come home occasionally. Then I told her she could retire, no more job. That did it! I accepted the offer and was informed I would be needed as soon as my responsibilities at Forest Lake were over. It was decided I would stay with Brent and Debby until Libby could finish her work at Forest Lake, then pack up and sell the house. This meant the Super Sport would come with us to Hinsdale. Brent and I could work together again!

I was aware that Brent had had intermittent back trouble. An occasional trip to a chiropractor seemed to relieve the problem. There had been x-rays and studies, and nothing was ever found to be a specific problem. We heard before I went north that the pain had increased, and an x-ray had revealed a small tumor. Brent and Debby had been informed by a surgeon that it was nothing to worry about. Ninety percent of tumors in this location were benign, and a brief surgical procedure would eliminate the problem. No sweat. The surgery was scheduled for early July. When I arrived in Hinsdale in late June Brent's pain was increasing almost hourly. Debby was alarmed and contacted the surgeon requesting that the procedure be moved up. She was told he planned to take a few days off and would consider it when he returned to work. The severe pain and strange sensations in his back and legs began on a Tuesday, and by Friday, Brent's pain was so severe he was admitted to the hospital. Many things were tried, and nothing was giving him relief. At this point, everyone was frustrated and frightened. Debby contacted the doctor and in no uncertain terms told him to get to the hospital, and get that tumor out. It was killing Brent!

The operation was to last about an hour. I had been in Illinois a week. One hour passed, then two, then three, then four. Debby is a registered nurse and knew something was terribly wrong. Finally, the surgeon and pathologist called us to a counseling room. The tumor had ruptured, which not only explained Brent's excruciating pain but also the time taken in the procedure to clean the mess in Brent's spinal cord. Pictures were produced, showing the wound before cleaning and after. The doctor tried to smile as he told Debby this could be a little more serious than first thought. I wasn't paying any attention to him. I was reading the eyes of the pathologist, who was keeping a stiff smile on his face, but his eyes told me this was major trouble. He knew what he had seen. My daughter also knew and was very clear to the surgeon that she knew the delay in surgery had contributed to the damage done to her husband's body.

Due to the deterioration in the tissue, the pathology lab in Hinsdale was unable to make a definite diagnosis, and so samples were sent to Johns Hopkins Medical Center in

Baltimore, Maryland, and the Mayo Clinic in Rochester, Minnesota. We were told to wait and see. At least now, the pain would be manageable and the surgeon said he felt he cleaned out all he could see.

For me, it was as if a sledgehammer had hit me in the stomach. I knew with brilliant clarity exactly why I had known months before I had to get out of teaching; why I had been drawn to chaplaincy; why against all odds I had been chosen by Hinsdale. I knew we were in for an intensive fight. I had no idea of the outcome, but I praised God that He had led Libby and me to the place we would need to be to support our family.

We learned the pathologists at Mayo and Johns Hopkins were friends and had been conferring with each other over Brent's diagnosis. The problem was, of course, the condition of the specimen. It was a month before they finally concluded it was probably an astrocytoma Stage 4, perhaps another similar kind. After a later surgery, the original diagnosis was changed to a form of medulloblastoma. Debby had gone to Hinsdale's medical library to research Brent's cancer diagnosis. The prognosis was anything but good. She informed us that only a handful of people lived beyond two years. Brent's disease was a rare, fast- growing, terribly aggressive cancer. But Brent was in excellent condition. At six foot, three inches, a marathon runner, surely his body could overcome this. Now we faced what countless families have faced. Brent would undergo chemotherapy, radiation, and the desperate search for a cure. Together, family and friends grasped our faith in prayer.

By August 1999, a second tumor had formed. All attempts to halt the progression of Brent's disease had been unsuccessful. What initially had seemed to be a problem of no particular consequence was now very clearly life threatening. Brent and Debby requested an anointing, and family and friends were invited to come together to join in prayer. Jonathan Leach was with us and led in our petitions. The Bible verses in the book of James so familiar to all of us were read: "Is any sick among you? Let him call for the elders of the church; and let them pray over him, anointing him with oil in the name of the Lord.

And the prayer of faith shall save the sick, and the Lord shall raise him up." James 5:14,15.

As I have in every anointing I have ever participated in, I explained to Brent there is no equivocation in these verses. You pray and place the oil on a person and the promise is they will be healed. The challenge I gave him has come back to haunt me. I told Brent that I knew of three ways the promise could be fulfilled: immediate healing; healing through medical science; healing through death and resurrection. I asked if he was willing to allow God to choose the way He wished to fulfill this promise. Brent readily answered in the affirmative and never looked back on his decision. Those in our group who chose to, prayed. Brent was anointed; within a few months after the operation he was a paraplegic.

So many diseases take away the quality of life piece by piece. We had hoped against hope that the damage to Brent's nerves due to surgery would heal. It was so painful to watch his desperate attempts to regain the use of his legs, but it was not to be. Brent had exactly a year left of life. In that time he would be in hospitals more than at home. The after-effects of aggressive treatment would bring him close to death several times. We never heard him ask the question, "Why me?"

Debby's struggle with Brent's care, concern for the children, and constant search for God's answers are best expressed in e-mails she sent periodically. The first two vignettes in this book involved Debby's faith. Now both she and Brent would need to draw on their faith constantly. Needless to say, her mother and I are very thankfully proud of her. The last six months of those e-mails follow.

* * *

June 24, 2000
Happy Sabbath!

We haven't sent any recent updates because there was really nothing new to report. Brent has been back at work and going to his physical therapy 3 times a week. He also had the intrathecal chemo every Thursday afternoon down at Evanston Hospital. This week was the last scheduled chemo.

Monday the 19th, he had an MRI of the brain as part of the routine follow-up. It is clear, and that is a big relief. Tuesday, he had an MRI of the spinal cord, and the report is "tumor is stable to slightly decreased." That, too, is good news, though we would have liked to hear it had decreased more or disappeared. Based on those results and the fact that Brent has had more than 8 weeks of continuous therapy, the doctor has recommended we repeat the MRI's in 4-6 weeks, and stay with no more chemo for now. Hopefully, the tumor will stay stable or decrease more while he takes a break.

Now for the setback: Thursday Brent ran a fever and showed signs of possible infection, so I took him to the ER to have a doctor look at him. He agreed that it looked like an infection and did blood cultures and started IV antibiotics. He was hospitalized at Hinsdale, and last night the blood cultures came back showing growth of bacteria, which means now he has another blood infection. That isn't good anytime, especially when a person has been on chemo for a long time, because the body can't fight it as well.

We were looking forward to sharing just good news this time and are disappointed to have to deal with another threat. His spirits are good, though this is hard for him to take. He wants so badly to just be free to work and be with our family. It has been a struggle for him to adjust to life in a wheelchair. He has done his best to do it with grace and hope that eventually he will walk again. But getting around buildings, restaurants, and stores in the wheelchair has had many challenges. Some places that are marked "Handicap Access" have obviously not had anyone in a wheelchair really there!

I am on my way in to be with him. I am relieved that he is in Hinsdale because he is 15 minutes away, not over an hour away. Also, we obviously know more people here, and the kids can have better access to him. Keep us in your prayers in a special way for this new challenge. This sinful world is really showing its ugly side these days it seems. We just need to have the strength to keep looking for God's face. I know He is there. I know He will be with us and Brent especially. We are praying for those of you who are in similar circumstances with your own pain and struggles.

We hope this day fills you with God's peace and that you enjoy time with your family, friends, and Creator. Love, Debby

* * *

July 1, 2000

Happy Sabbath!

Brent continues in the hospital with the infection. He has a large abscess on his hip that the doctors are keeping a close eye on with frequent dressing changes and evaluations. He is at greater risk for complications from all the chemotherapy and radiation. This is a very serious illness, and it will be awhile before he is out of the woods. He is feeling better, though, and the blood infection is clearing up. Now that he is feeling better, it is harder for him to stay in bed!

Brent's brother Ron flew in yesterday morning after a grueling flight! Brent and I had just been saying it would be nice to have someone to help keep him company when I was tending to the children. Right after we talked, Ron called to say he was coming! That's an example of what it says in the Bible "before they call, I will answer!" We are so happy to have him here. The kids mobbed him upon his arrival and have made plans for some of his time.

I don't know if I mentioned our new puppy in the last letter. His name is "Rusty" and he is an Australian Shepherd. He is 9 weeks old and very smart and sweet. The children have been promised a dog for at least 3 years, and with the move and fighting cancer, there never seemed to be the right time. He is the color they had chosen long ago, and was nearby at a good time with summer vacation coming up. We are enjoying him and he is giving a positive focus to help with some of the difficulties we have encountered with Brent's illness.

Have a good day with your families. We appreciate your prayers and letters. Thank you for your faithfulness in bringing us before God.

Love, Debby

* * *

July 29, 2000

Happy Sabbath!

Brent is finally home! Yesterday, the 28th, after 5 long weeks, he was able to leave the hospital. Of course, the air conditioner decided to quit, and the special airbed delivery was delayed, and that threw the whole day off! I suggested to him that if he wanted supper, he better eat it there. He did and we arrived home at 7:45 pm. Then, upon getting into the special airbed, it promptly went flat! So I blew up an air mattress while waiting for the company to come fix the bed, and then he ended up sleeping on it the whole night because the guy couldn't fix the problem. Today we had a new one delivered and the jury is still out on whether it is working correctly. Isn't it just one thing after another?

Last night amidst all the comings and goings, I went into the living room where the kids were wrestling loudly and the dogs were barking and suggested that they keep it down a little. After all, I said, Daddy just got home from a very quiet place where everyone was helpful. Andrew asked, "Did Daddy want to come home?" I said, "Of course," and he replied, "Well, this is what home is like!" Out of the mouths of babes! They wanted to know what the night nurse was doing there, how long she would stay and why. They were afraid of her intruding into their space. She quickly won them over and was very helpful with Brent. She will be helping at night for a while so I can get some sleep. The puppy gave

Brent "welcome home" gifts all over the place, so I guess he felt intruded upon too!

Brent still has a long way to go in his recovery. The wound hasn't healed yet and will take some time. He is having some steroid withdrawal symptoms that hopefully will disappear this week or next. I think that the stimulation of home will help him, but the food may not be as well scheduled! Taco Bell is just down the road in case of emergency. We are trying to feed him a high-protein, low-fat diet. He has lost a lot of strength from the prolonged bed rest and will have therapists coming to the house twice a day to help him regain mobility. He has to stay out of the wheelchair except for short transfers until he heals.

Brent's dad was here for 2 weeks and just left last Tuesday. He was such a help and so faithful in his care of Brent. He really demonstrates love in action with his involvement in every aspect of Brent's care. I was touched this time as always at how he was willing to do whatever it took to help Brent. He was by Brent's side for most of the day, and I know he got tired, too. We are blessed to have caring Christian parents. They are helping us through this, and I don't know what we'd do without them. The emotional support is comforting. Brent's sister Karen and her son Ryan are coming next week. The kids are looking forward to having some cool teenager taking them around instead of just Mom! Andrew will turn 10 on the 2nd and is happy Dad is home for his birthday.

Brent is busy figuring out how to do business from home, and I am trying to make him balance it with his therapy as a priority. There are no easy answers, but hopefully we will meet both needs. We see his neuro-oncologist in a couple of weeks, and he will have MRI's then to check on the tumor status.

Keep us in your prayers as always. It is not easy to "In all things give thanks, for this is the will of the Father concerning you." I struggle with maintaining a positive attitude after really long days of caregiving, then am rescued by the Holy Spirit reminding me of all the blessings we have. Daily we are given the strength to meet the challenges in our path, just as manna came down from heaven to the Israelites. Just enough for the day, not the week or month. I am learning to live in the moment and feel peace and joy no matter what is happening.

Have a good week. May God help you with your challenges.

Love, Debby

* * *

September 16, 2000

Happy Sabbath!

So much has happened since the last letter. It seems some days that events are moving at light speed. Thursday, the 7th, we re-admitted Brent to the hospital with nausea that we couldn't control. We then spent the next few days adjusting medications for the nausea and pain, and testing to find a cause. We found that the tumor has grown significantly, though it is still in the spinal cord, not in the brain. We have consulted with doctors here and other places, and they all are in agreement that any more aggressive treatment will do more harm to Brent than good.

Tuesday, I took 24 hours to stay home waiting for phone calls, to pray, to cry, to yell on occasion. My mom took the kids, and Brent's sister Karen stayed with him. On Wednesday morning, the doctor who had been with us treating this for a year finally called. She concurred with the other doctors that though we had put up a good fight, this tumor is terribly aggressive and Hospice care would give him the best quality of life for what time he has left. Even discussing Hospice has given me nausea and dizziness! But I felt after much prayer, asking all our doctors and even some others, that this illness has always been in God's hands, will continue to be, and the most important thing is to keep Brent comfortable with what is a very painful illness. He is actually more able to visit with us now that he is more medicated.

Yesterday, we brought him home from the hospital. The Hospice nurse and social worker spent a lot of time with us getting everything settled and comfortable. He had a good night with Karen acting as the night nurse. We hope and pray for a lot of good nights. Brent's parents went home for a few days, but are back with us. It is comforting to both of us for them to be here. They are so helpful, and Brent asks for his dad first thing in the morning. Fortunately, Dad Edgerton is an early riser, and I am able to sleep a little better!

Many of you have mentioned coming for a visit. Right now, he actually visits better by phone. The nausea arises suddenly and unpredictably, and visits are interrupted. We are trying to keep his energy for positive family interaction with the children, me, and his folks, and siblings. We appreciate your concerns and prayers; phone calls and e-mails are great. I am being protective of the needs of Brent, myself, and the children. He tires very easily, and his comfortable talkative moments are special. They are also very few and far between. They need to be preserved for the special memories that my children have of great times with their daddy. Brent enjoys reminiscing about old times with good friends, but at this time, it is best done by phone.

We are resting in the hope of a new earth where our tears will be wiped away and our bodies will be made new. I talked with the children Wednesday night about what Hospice means, about the new findings for Daddy's tumor, and that we can't do anything medically to change things. They cried, then said they have a great daddy and are glad they have had him, cause so many kids don't have a good one. They ended with laughter and good memories, and prayers for healing, but at the same time accepting God's will and peace with whatever comes. Brent and I pray that they will continue to seek the comfort of the Holy Spirit for whatever storms they encounter in life. The Hospice people said the kids seem remarkably well adjusted and normal with what has been such a stressful 16 months.

We thank you for your prayers. We are hurting but focusing on maintaining Brent's health in the best way we can and seeking God's peace. May you be comforted in your own trials during this week.

Love, Debby

* * *

October 9, 2000

Dear Friends and Family,

Sabbath was a happy Sabbath. Our 10-year-old son Andrew was baptized by his grandfather. Brent was able to view it later via video tape.   We are pleased that Andrew made the choice to give his heart to God and was also able to share it with his father. I had forgotten in all that is going on that he has been studying toward that goal, and he and my dad reminded me last week and we made the plans. Uncles Ron, Kevin, and Rick were here and Aunt Karen.

I'm writing tonight to let you know that Brent is in the process of dying now. My heart is breaking. His mother and sister are here, the children have been here throughout the day, and they have said their goodby's and we are playing his favorite music. He is struggling, and I am asking you to read this and pray for peace and rest for him. He has fought so well and hard. So please lift us up especially to the Lord as we face this last battle.

Thank you for your help. It will comfort us as we think of your prayers on our behalf. I will let you know how the blessings unfold.

Love, Debby

* * *

Dear Friends and Family,

Brent passed away at 11:20 pm on October 9, 2000. The memorial will probably be Thursday. Thank you for your prayers. I'll write more later.

Love, Debby

* * *

Dear Friends and Family,

We have decided on the Memorial Service for Brent. It will be on Friday, October 13 at 1:30 pm in the Hinsdale Seventh-day Adventist Church. The address is: 201 N. Oak Street, Hinsdale, IL 60521. The interment is yet to be decided.

In lieu of flowers, there is a memorial fund set up through the Hinsdale Hospital Foundation. Their address is: 7 Salt Creek Suite #203, Hinsdale, IL 60521. Brent was involved in several projects at his Bolingbrook facility, and the Executive team and employees are deciding on the best project to bear his name. I will let you know the exact one that is chosen.

We are holding onto each other and to the Lord. Actually, He is holding onto us right now. Nothing makes sense, but it doesn't have to. We are walking through the Valley of the Shadow of Death, and He will help us to fear no evil.

Love, Debby

* * *

Dear Friends and Family,

I haven't written since the memorial notice, and many of you have inquired to see if things are going o.k. Well, things are going along as they must, I suppose. We are all exhausted, both emotionally and physically. Chrissy has been running a high temp for the past few nights, so I've been up with her. Tonight, Andrew complained that his throat is hurting too. So the count is rising! The kids have all been sleeping in my room, so we are sharing germs in close quarters. Hopefully, tonight we might get some rest. Eric seems to be o.k., but does have a headache. The counselors have warned us about the possibility of getting sick after so much stress. Better bring out the Vitamin C.

Brent's Memorial on October 13 was lovely. The music was well done, with some of our friends getting together a quartet to do some of Brent's favorite Cathedral Quartet music. Andy McDonald did a beautiful sermon, and Brent's brother Ron bravely and beautifully sang. We had wanted it to be a witness, not only for Brent's life, but for our faith as well, and I think that was accomplished. Several of our neighbors came, and have come over to say they were so touched, so we can pray the Holy Spirit keeps working. Several of our friends and family were here to help carry us through, and their love and counsel were greatly appreciated. I had thought that I was prepared, but I'm not sure now you ever can be. It hurts more with each passing day, because the memories of Brent before the illness get stronger and stronger. Almost like now that the "sick Brent is gone", where is the "well Brent"? When is he going to call and come home? I keep thinking I hear the car pulling in the drive, and his footsteps. But no.

The feelings of helplessness are overwhelming, so it is easier to be angry at everything; big or small, it doesn't seem to matter. Last week, I spent most of the time in bed, trying to sleep or crying. I kept thinking it had to stop, but it sure took a long time to slow down. And where was the peace that God had provided so wonderfully during so much of Brent's illness? It has taken awhile to "seek peace and pursue it." What the anger has taught me, though, is that God knew how I would feel, He knew that Brent would die, and how I would react, and He still sent the peace before when I begged for it. He has taught me to be more accepting of others' anger at God's provisions (or seeming lack of) because He can handle it! He can even use it. So, I can't remember now if the next phase of the Grief process is Depression or Bargaining, but whatever it is, God knows about it and will be with me. I think it may be Depression, because when I don't feel angry, I feel depressed! My mom has been reminding me to "smile, and calm down."

Please continue to remember us in your prayers. Even though the last months were hard, it is harder to continue on without Brent. None of us want to go into the family room where he spent his last weeks. We want him to be there to at least touch. There are so many questions throughout the day, and I want to do what's best. Pray that God will "guide me and teach me in the way that I should go." Thank you for your support.

Love, Debby

* * *

After Brent's death, I had no more heart to continue re-building the Super Sport. It was sold.

~ Chapter Six ~

Hospice: The Holy Spirit And The Terminally Ill

A few weeks before Brent's death, an opening for a chaplain with St. Thomas Hospice became available. I had become interested in the work of Hospice due to observing the expertise and dedication given to patients who were referred by the hospital to hospice care. St. Thomas Hospice (begun by a mother who lost her son Thomas to cancer) was a subsidiary of Hinsdale Adventist Hospital. I applied and was accepted. Shortly after it was realized Brent was terminal he was referred to St. Thomas.

When the admitting nurse met with Debby, the available hospice services were explained to her. Each hospice recipient must accept a nurse and social worker; all other services, including chaplain, are optional. When asked if the services of a chaplain were desired, Debby answered yes. When my name was suggested, Debby immediately stated I couldn't be used. Red flags immediately went up and she was asked to explain. Debby replied, "He's my dad!" We found someone else.

You will hear the word "palliative" used extensively in the work of hospice. The World Health Organization defines palliative care in these words: "The active total care of patients whose disease is not responsive to curative treatment. Control of pain, of other symptoms, and of psychological, social, and spiritual problems is paramount. The goal of palliative care is achievement of the best possible quality of life for patients and their families" (World Health Organization, CANCER PAIN RELIEF AND PALLIATIVE CARE, Technical Report 804).

Pioneered in England, hospice took root in the United States during the 1970s. Hospice care was initially designed for people who were dying of cancer, and who had a functional family support system and a home where they could be cared for away from the high-tech hospital environment. It soon was to include not only cancer, but terminal illness, no matter what the cause. As awareness for the needs of the dying grew, it became apparent that palliative care was essential, regardless of age or financial condition. This awareness culminated in hospice being included in the Medicare program in 1983.

The specific needs of dying persons to which care must respond can be grouped under the headings of physical, emotional, and social well-being. Within each category, the health care system plays an important role in meeting these needs but is never the only actor and not always even the chief actor. Physical needs include a safe, clean, and comfortable place for dying; control of pain and symptoms; appropriate food and nutrition; personal care (aid with bathing, feeding, dressing, and other activities of daily living); information about how best to manage the physical condition of the dying person; and information about the changes in physical condition to be expected over time. Emotional needs include respect for the dying person's dignity as a human being; respect for the dying person's wishes to the extent possible; information about the emotional changes to expect; counseling to help the patient come to terms with what is happening; assistance with advance planning for death; and attending to spiritual concerns. Social needs include companionship; maintenance of social functioning, to the extent possible; assistance in "telling one's life story" to others; and help in resolving relationships and taking care of other "unfinished business."

A few months after Brent's death, Debby told her mother and me she had to go back home to central Florida. We told her she had a beautiful home near Hinsdale and wonderful friends, was she sure? She replied, "This house is a death house to me. Brent became ill here, for months we cared for him here, and he died here. Every time I go into that room, it all comes back!"

I immediately told her she wasn't ready to fly on her own. If she had to return to Florida, I would resign from St.

Thomas, and we would go with her. We knew she and the children would need our close support. Debby informed us we could live anywhere in Florida we wished as long as it wasn't over fifteen minutes away. We returned home, Debby purchased a home, and we bought one five miles away on two acres of land (room to re-establish Libby's nursery).

As the time approached for our move, I had been unable to find work. Two weeks before we left Hinsdale, a friend, Don Hires, called, "Larry, I hear you're coming back to Florida. Do you have a job?"

I replied, "No."

He continued, "How would you like to work as a hospice chaplain here?"

Don was working as a chaplain for Hospice of Lake and Sumter Counties with headquarters only a few miles from our new home. I applied and was accepted.

When old friends ask what I'm doing and I reply I am a hospice chaplain, so many times I see a look of pity. It's so hard to explain what a joy, honor, and privilege it is to shepherd people and their families through this crucial stage in life all of us must face. In forty-nine years of ministry I have never had more challenging, yes, and exciting, and rewarding work. Allow me to give a few examples:

Bill

The presence of the Holy Spirit is so close in this work. Bill was an eighty-six-year-old with both a defibulator and a pacemaker. Although Bill's heart was shot, it didn't affect his sense of humor one bit, and I enjoyed his company immensely. He loved a good clean joke, and we certainly laughed at our share, but Bill's faith in Christ was uppermost. The communions we shared were among the most reverent I have ever experienced.

I was headed in one direction and almost at my destination when that Divine Presence spoke in His unique way. The instruction was that I was to turn around and Bill's name came to mind. Immediately that about-face was maneuvered, and I headed ten miles in the opposite direction. I don't even recall ringing the doorbell or knocking; I walked in and found Bill ashen-faced, his lips blue. He was in excruciating pain in the throes of a heart attack. Bill lived alone, and as you can imagine I needed medical advice immediately. I called his hospice nurse and received the instruction I needed to administer nitroglycerine and morphine, then called 911. As Bill was being wheeled out on a gurney, he looked at me and asked how I knew he needed me. I could only reply that Jesus told me. Bill lived another six months. I've wondered why that few months were so important to Bill and God that the Spirit gave me such urgent instruction. Whatever it was, I hope Bill used the time to work it out.

Ruth

When our admitting nurse first met Ruth and asked if she wanted a chaplain, Ruth's reply was, "I don't want no (expletive deleted) preacher in my house!" You can imagine my surprise when a couple of weeks later a nurse told me Ruth had requested a chaplain, but there was to be "no prayers and I don't want to be preached to!"

This certainly was unusual. I have received such invitations a few times since, but this was my first. Just the title, Chaplain, carries with it a certain expectation of spiritual care. Hopefully, I have learned to respect a persons faith, or even lack of it. An individual may be Christian, Buddhist, Hindu, Moslem, Jew. I have even met one devotee of Zoroaster. In respect to faiths other than Christian, I make sure prayers are directed toward the Creator; the name of Jesus won't be used unless it is requested.

So, I faced Ruth's door with a little trepidation. I was asked in, and soon Ruth and I were in a lively discussion about trips, former jobs, children, and grand- children. I learned Ruth had been married to the same man three times. I asked her why she divorced him the second time. She said, "Oh, I was going through the menopause, got mad at him, and threw him out!" Ruth was a character. The next few visits went the same, but the Holy Spirit was nudging me pretty hard that I needed to give more spiritual guidance. So I decided that at the next visit, even if Ruth threw me out, I would at least ask if I could pray with her. Soon I was sitting across from my friend, enjoying our time together and trying to get up the courage to make my request. All of a sudden Ruth pointed to a book on an end table. She said, "Larry, I want you to pick up that book and look through it." As I did, I began reading the wonderful promises of salvation, forgiveness, and God's love. I looked at Ruth and asked, "Ruth, do you believe this?" She looked at me, smiled, and replied, "Well, (expletive deleted) I better start believing in something; I'm about to die!"

I learned that her granddaughter was a devout Christian, and knowing her grandmother's spiritual condition, she had given her grandmother the book. I was so honored to confirm Ruth's faith in Jesus and finally have that prayer. Two days later, Ruth died.

Ruth was one of my first hospice patients and she taught me so much. Never again have I felt pressured to work toward any spiritual agenda. I learned that if I could develop rapport with patients, once they had gained confidence in me, if there were spiritual concerns, they would be brought forth.

The Wedding Ring

Karen was eighty-two and dying of liver cancer. Until her illness, she had been the CEO of her own business. Karen had a hot temper and would lose it at the drop of a hat. She usually dropped the hat. As can be imagined, she and her husband Mel had had a volatile relationship, but as I visited with this couple, it was evident they loved each other deeply. So many times I explain to loved ones of the terminally ill that they aren't caring for the person they have known. Disease and strong medication cause psychological changes that hurt those close by. Language used and hateful attitudes that are completely out of character for a person may be manifested. As Karen's illness progressed, this seemed to be the case.

I was paged to go to Karen's side due to a conflict between her and Mel. When I arrived, Karen was glaring at Mel and clutched in her hand his wedding band. Mel was in tears and explained that Karen had recalled an incident that had caused her hurt and demanded he give her the ring. Karen wouldn't tell what all this was about, and it was evident she was in no mood to discuss the situation. The eyes and body language may indicate to a degree what is in a person's mind, but the only Being who can accurately read a human mind is the Holy Spirit. In every encounter I have, there is a three-way conversation taking place: that individual and me, and at the same time my petition to the Spirit for assistance to know how I can be of help. As this process continued with Karen, the solution to the problem was revealed. Karen was Catholic and the Lord's Prayer (the "Our Father") had been very special to her since she was a small child. I asked Karen to repeat it with me, but after each phrase I asked her to explain what it meant to her. We had only gone through two phrases ("Our Father which art in heaven and hallowed be Thy name") when Karen realized where we were heading. She cut those hazel eyes at me and if they had been daggers, she would have nailed me to the wall. But she was trapped. She didn't want to continue, but she couldn't stop a prayer that meant so much to her. Then we came to, "and forgive us our trespasses <u>as we forgive those who trespass against us.</u>" Before I could ask for her meaning of these words, Karen said, "Larry Stephens, You are the biggest rascal I ever let in the house! Don't you say a word!" Now it was the Spirit's turn to do the work only He can do. I stayed quiet while Karen faced the Author of her prayer. After a few minutes her features softened and she said, "I forgive you, Mel." And she handed back the ring.

Janet

Janet was driving everyone in the household crazy. In the final stages of cancer that was in every major organ, she refused to go to sleep. Lights were on and the television was blaring all hours of the day and night, and Janet kept going by the sheer force of her will. When I arrived at her home, she had just lain down on her bed.

Janet had the most beautiful blue eyes I have ever seen, and as she looked at me, all I could see was defiance. I introduced myself and asked if I could visit. Janet motioned to a chair close by.

Janet explained that she had been verbally and physically abused by her husband and finally abandoned with five small children. She told of the struggle she had faced to raise her three boys and two girls by herself. I was impressed to ask where the children were and what they were doing. I learned one of the boys was a medical doctor, another was in medical school, the third son was attending the Michigan Institute of Technology (MIT), one daughter was a nurse, and the other, a teacher. I sat back in amazement and said, "I'm looking at one tough Mama! To have faced the adversity you have and yet raised those children to be such credits to society is so commendable. You must be very thankful and proud!"

For the first time, those eyes softened and she smiled. Then she explained that was the problem; her mother's heart couldn't find a way to leave her children and grandchildren. What was to become of them? She stated she was angry at God and thought it was terribly unfair that she would soon be deprived of her family. I explained that God has big shoulders and was not turned off by our anger. He realizes when things get rough that we might question the path he has placed us on. But He constantly reminds us that He is walking that path with us, and He invites us to talk it out with Him. We began to discuss her faith and God's guidance in our lives and the lives of those we love. Finally, I asked if she would like to have communion. After a moment's thought, she said she would appreciate that very much; it had been so long since her last. Libby and I had traded vehicles for the day and my communion material was in the other car. I explained this and was about to make an appointment for the next day when the Spirit stepped in and told me in no uncertain terms I didn't have that kind of time. I told Janet I would get what was needed and be back in a few minutes. Grape juice and Wheat Thins were purchased at a market, a cup was borrowed from Janet's daughter and we were ready. As the service ended, Janet's eyes showed such relief and exhaustion. As I do in so many homes, I asked if I could give her a kiss on the forehead before I left. A wan smile and a nod gave consent. That kiss means so much. It is an acknowledgement that a person is so very valued and accepted. Janet's daughter told me later that as soon as I left the room, her mother went to sleep. Two hours later she was gone. That kiss had been her final good night.

Rob and Mary

As I approached the front porch, Mary was sitting at a patio table crying. Well, this wasn't so unusual. Her husband had just been told his lung cancer was terminal. I sat at the table and soon learned Mary's tears weren't just for her husband. She and Rob, the man I had thought was her husband, had lived together unmarried for twenty-seven years.

Ken was Rob's son-in-law from his first marriage, and Ken had his eyes on Rob's twenty-five acres of prime land fenced for horses and with a fine barn adjacent to the house. Ken's livelihood was caring for and training horses. This land was to become the basis for his business. Ken had informed Mary she had no rights to Rob's property since they weren't married, and as soon as Rob died, she would have to leave. Ken had illegally obtained a power of attorney and subsequently removed all documents from the home and changed all the locks so as to have access to any part of the property, including the home. He had removed all of the money from their bank account; confiscated Rob's very valuable gun collection; and was now intent on bullying Mary so as to make her as uncomfortable as possible.

Mary was devoted to Rob and cared for him faithfully day and night. Consequently, she was exhausted. Ken used Mary's exhaustion to his advantage by browbeating her at every opportunity when he found the slightest thing that didn't meet his approval. ("Don't you ever dust this shelf!?"---"When do you plan to do the dishes!?"—"The pasture needs cutting!! When are you going to see to it!?") This would continue at any hour, day or night. Ken had a violent past and hadn't physically abused Mary yet, but his temper and attitude had her terrified. Mary had held a job for years to help pay for their home and property, but this was not to be considered.

There was such a simple solution. (You're probably way ahead of me on this.) I asked Mary why she and Rob didn't get married. Rob was still lucid and under Florida law, a home and property that were paid for couldn't be taken from the spouse. Mary's countenance lit up. I honestly don't think she had even considered this.

Just as I was leaving, Ken drove up. Tall and muscular, he was the picture of arrogant self-assurance. He couldn't wait to lay out to me his plans for the land he was looking at. I couldn't help thinking this young, arrogant man just might be in for an extremely abrupt and painfully rude awakening. When asked about Mary, he assured me she had children who would probably care for her.

A week later I was asked to come to Rob and Mary's home. Rob asked if I would marry them. I told them I would arrange it but would find an officer of the County Court to perform the ceremony. I was concerned that the marriage might be contested, and I knew if a court officer performed the ceremony, there would be a check on Rob's mental acumen that would become part of the court records.

When I went to the courthouse to arrange for a license, I found that Rob and Mary's social security cards and a picture identification for both were required. Rob's wallet with his driver's license had been taken, along with other personal records. We were allowed to use income tax records for Rob's social security number. Rob was very weak, but I was able to load him into my truck, take him to the local department of motor vehicles, and, as his driver's license was on record, obtain a picture ID. A young lady who was an officer of the court agreed to go to the home and help complete the marriage license. Later I stood with Rob and Mary as a court officer first tested Rob's competency and then performed the service. I told Mary to immediately change all locks; obtain an attorney; get a court order banning the son-in-law from the property; and have everything that had been taken illegally returned.

Soon the money was back in the bank; guns were home; all documents (including the wallet) returned. A few days later, I witnessed Rob's new will that made sure Mary was cared for. The next morning Mary woke to find Rob had died in his sleep.

From time to time I would check on Mary, just to make sure she was alright. The last time I was with her, she had just returned from a trip to Hawaii with her grandchildren. I can't find words to express how rewarding it was to watch Mary's metamorphosis from a sobbing victim to a woman empowered to be in control of her affairs.

Ada

Ada was raised in a Christian home. When her mother died suddenly, Ada was so devastated and confused that she turned against God and at eighteen left home. She soon found herself on the street with bad companions and no means of support. Ada became addicted to drugs and alcohol and turned to prostitution. Her father Al was a former marine tank commander whose body bore the scars of hand-to-hand combat. Jesus had changed Al, and he was determined to find his daughter, if at all possible.

Five years went by with no word of Ada. By this time her body was destroyed by her lifestyle of abuse. A customer left her at an emergency room more dead than alive. The medical staff soon decided there was nothing they could do. Ada's liver and immune system were destroyed. Someone contacted Al and told him of his daughter's location and condition. Al found her and took her home.

Ada was so weak she couldn't hold her head up. Al began caring for her as if she were again an infant. This tough, scarred, former marine would raise her up with one hand and feed her with the other. He told me later he prayed with every bite that God would not only save her physically but, far more importantly, save her spiritually. Gradually Ada gained strength. Al's devotion impressed Ada to turn again to Jesus. After she was able, she began attending church and was nurtured by a loving Christian community.

As could be expected, Ada had many questions as she grew in Jesus, especially about prayer. Al decided to write out his answers and in all I have read about prayer, I have never found a better explanation than Al's letter to his daughter:

"DOES PRAYER CHANGE THINGS?"

They say that prayer changes things, but does it REALLY change anything?

Oh yes! It really does!

Does prayer change your present situation or sudden circumstances?

No, not always, but it does change the way you look at those events.

Does prayer change your financial future?

No, not always, but it does change whom you look to for meeting your daily needs.

Does prayer change shattered hearts or broken bodies?

No, not always, but it will change your source of strength and comfort.

Does prayer change your wants and desires?

No, not always, but it will change your wants into what God desires!

Does prayer change how you view the world?

No, not always, but it will change whose eyes you see the world through.

Does prayer change your regrets from the past?

No, not always, but it will change your hopes for the future!

Does prayer change the people around you?

No, not always, but it will change you; the problem isn't always in others.

Does prayer change your life in ways you can't explain?

Oh, yes, always! And it will change you from the inside out!

So does prayer REALLY change ANYTHING?

Yes! It REALLY does change EVERYTHING!

Due to the lack of an immune system, a liver transplant is out of the question. Ada has come to us at Hospice and is terminal. Each time I meet with her, I am so impressed by not only her faith, but for her loving determination to help others.

The Golden Angel

Each Christmas I hang a small gold-colored angel ornament on the tree. Bruce was thirty-eight years old. A type-I diabetic, he had lost a foot, and his kidneys were failing as well as his eyesight. He had been informed that in order to live, he must go on dialysis. Bruce said no. He had fought his disease all his life, and he wanted no more treatment. As I met with him over the weeks, I was so amazed at his upbeat attitude, not only toward life but toward death as well. There was no pity, and he wouldn't put up with any manifested around him. Just before Christmas, he asked me to close my eyes and put out my hand. I was by this time very familiar with Bruce's penchant for practical jokes and honored his request with some trepidation. When I looked at what was placed there, I saw that gold-colored angel Christmas tree ornament. Bruce told me he had asked the Lord to let him be a guardian angel, and he intended to watch over me for the rest of my life. The angel was a gift to remind me of his promise. With that twinkle in his eyes I had become so familiar with, he added, 'That, of course, means you'll have to behave!' Maybe his theology was questionable, but not his intent.

I keep Bruce's angel in a special box. As I said before, each Christmas it has an honored place on our tree. Bruce will be with us always.

Dee

As you have probably ascertained from this chapter, I am constantly blessed by the evidence of the Holy Spirit in the lives of those I serve. Dee certainly provided her share of those blessings. Shortly before she died, she wrote the following prayer. As I read it, the depth of her insight and the stunning beauty of her poetic expression lifted my spirit into the Master's presence.

(In order to reproduce Dee's prayer as closely as possible to the way she wrote it, we have placed it on the following page.)

Dee's Prayer

Dear God......
Please help me walk in your light
and remind me that I am
a beautiful rose in the bouquet
of your divinity
and that my mountainous
problems are just temporary.
Teach me compassion,
remind me that my words
and my speech contain great power,
and to use them with good intentions.
Tap me on the shoulder
when I make assumptions.
Help me to love unconditionally
and refrain from judging.
I surrender my burden and
lay it at your feet, dear God.
Thank you for taking it from me.

C. D. Beighey

~ Chapter Seven ~

Connecting With The Covenant

In the previous pages, I have tried to explain just a little of what it has meant to my family and me to accept and follow God's Covenant. There is a direct connection between the Covenant as taught by Jesus and the warning we as Seventh-day Adventists refer to as the Third Angel's Message. This chapter is devoted to exploring the Covenant. Chapter Nine is devoted to explaining that direct connection to God's last message to humanity.

"God is love." I John 4:8. From the beginning, the Trinity was determined that love would be the dominant Theme of all creation. The problem with love is that love has the potential, not only for the greatest good but also for the greatest harm. Love must be based on the unrestricted freedom of choice. We choose to love. God knew if love was to dominate, this freedom not only could, but eventually would turn against Him. Sin would come. For this reason Jesus chose to be the "Lamb slain from the foundation of the world." Why?

We have all become familiar more or less with computers. We know a virus can be developed that destroys various computer functions. A virus always has a specific purpose. The human mind is the greatest computer. Lucifer began the rebellion foreseen by God. After being cast out of heaven, he was determined to continue his war with God on earth by attacking God's special creation, man. With Lucifer's vastly superior intellect, second only to the Trinity, he knew if he could gain the allegiance of Adam for just a moment, he could inject a virus into the human mind that would be passed to all future generations. The purpose of this virus we call sin was to eventuate in the elimination of humanity. Through hatred and greed, we would destroy ourselves. This is the background of the third chapter of Genesis. The last six thousand years have demonstrated the effectiveness of Satan's plan, but for Jesus.

As God and man, Jesus came to live the life we couldn't live and then die our death, even the death of the cross. By entering into covenant with Him and accepting that life, we give Him the right to remove the virus.

"… We will all be changed. In a flash, in the twinkling of an eye, at the last trumpet. For the trumpet will sound, the dead will be raised imperishable, and we will be changed. For the perishable must clothe itself with the imperishable, and the mortal with immortality. When the perishable has been clothed with the imperishable and the mortal with immortality, then the saying that is written will come true: 'Death has been swallowed up in victory.' "

"Where, O death, is your victory? Where, O hades, is your sting? The sting of death is sin, ..."   1 Corinthians 15:51-56. NIV

The virus is removed!

How many people will be saved? The Bible describes the number of saved in these words: "After this I saw a **great multitude that no man could number** of all nations, and kindred, and people, and tongues, standing before the throne, and before the Lamb, in white robes with palms in their hands" Revelation 7: 9.

Many people have the idea that very few will be saved, but the Scriptures don't uphold this view at all. The Bible declares the saved are as numberless as the stars of heaven (Genesis 15:5), the dust of the earth (Genesis 13:6), and the sand of the sea (Genesis 22: 17). Imagine, hundreds of millions of God's children redeemed from this earth! We wonder how many deserve this privilege, and Scripture answers:

"But we are all as an unclean thing, and all our righteousness is as a filthy rag; and we all fade as a leaf, and our sins, like the wind, have taken us away" Isaiah 64: 6.

Paul says:

"For we have proved before that both Jews and

Gentiles are all under sin; as it is written, there is no one righteous, no, not one" Romans 3:9, 10.

The lowest common denominator of the human race is that all of us are sinners in desperate need of grace! We begin the explanation of how all these millions of undeserving people get to heaven by studying Titus 2:13, 14: "Looking for that blessed hope, and the glorious appearing of the great God and our Savior Jesus Christ; Who gave Himself for us, that He might **redeem us** from all iniquity, and **purify** unto Himself a peculiar people, zealous of good works."

Notice that Jesus came to **redeem** and **purify** man. This twofold process of **redemption** and **purification** is the theme of all the Bible. Every word of God's Book is written to explain or illustrate either one or both of these two principles. The Covenant explains how Jesus accomplishes this.

If I want to understand my Covenant with Jesus, I want to get it directly from Him, not secondhand. In the third chapter of John's gospel is the most important conversation ever recorded on earth. I want to encourage you to take a moment to read the account before continuing. This will enable you to place the following outline in context. In Christ's encounter with Nicodemus, we find His agreement with us consists of four parts.

THE COVENANT, Part One — JOHN 3:16

"For God so loved the world, that He gave His only

begotten Son that whosoever believes in Him should not perish, but have everlasting life."

As in all agreements, John 3:16 reveals that both God and man have responsibilities. **Our responsibility is to accept Jesus as our personal Savior. God's responsibility is to give us at that moment of that acceptance everlasting life, immediate entry into the Kingdom of God as His son or daughter.**

A note of caution: Scripture explains that the everlasting life given in John 3:16 is **conditional.** I am not given immortality until the return of Jesus (1 Corinthians 15: 51-53). In order for the everlasting life of John, chapter 3, to become the immortality of 1 Corinthians, chapter 15, I must stay with Jesus.

THE COVENANT, Part Two: The New Birth — JOHN 3: 5, 6

"Jesus answered, Truly, I tell you, except a man is born of water and the Spirit, he cannot enter the kingdom of God. That which is born of the flesh is flesh; and that which is born of the Spirit is spirit."

At the moment of my acceptance of Jesus as Savior, the new birth takes place: the bonding of my mind with the Holy Spirit. This miracle, **the union of the mind of God with the mind of man,** can't be explained or understood. Jesus said:

"Don't marvel that I told you, you must be born again. The wind blows where it wishes, you hear the sound, but you can't tell where it comes from or where it goes. So is everyone who is born of the Spirit" John 3: 7,8.

In the new birth the Great Creator uses the awesome power that formed our universe to come into our hearts. In another of those references to be used again, Paul said: "For we are His workmanship, created in Christ Jesus for good works, which God prepared beforehand that we should walk in them" Ephesians 2: 10.

Satan's placing of the virus, sin, based on his knowledge that the mind is a computer doesn't compare to the Creator's internet connection to the brain. The new birth gives the Holy Spirit access to those spiritual neurons we call the conscience. For centuries Hebrews 8: 10 has stated:

"For this is the covenant that I will make with the house of Israel after those days, says the Lord: I will put my laws in their mind and write them on their hearts: ..."

Now, knowing that the brain is a computer, we can understand the real significance of the words, "write them in our hearts." As we all know, the "heart" doesn't refer to our blood pump, but the conscience. Upon accepting Jesus, The Holy Spirit immediately begins to program the mind to think God's way by establishing the precepts of the Decalogue. This not only begins our growth in Christ we call sanctification, but opens the way for the fruit of the Spirit listed by Paul:

"...love, joy, peace, longsuffering, kindness, goodness, faithfulness, gentleness, self-control, against such there is no law." Galatians 5 22,23

Notice in the following list of texts that every connection between God and each of us is controlled by the direct communication with our minds by the Holy Spirit:

He:

- Interprets our prayers -- Romans 8: 26, 27
- Testifies of Jesus -- John 15: 26
- Guides us into all truth -- John 16: 13
- Makes us witnesses -- 11 Corinthians 3: 3-6
- Gives us words to say -- Luke 12: 11,12
- Fills our hearts with the love of God -- Romans 5:5
- Seals us -- Ephesians 1: 13
- Guarantees our inheritance -- Ephesians 1: 14

This chain will be broken at this point in order to highlight the two gifts found in Ephesians 1:13,14: "In whom you also trusted after you heard the word of truth, the gospel of your salvation: in whom after you believed **you were sealed with that Holy Spirit of promise."**

The sealing work of the Holy Spirit will be studied in more detail. For now I would emphasize being sealed by the Spirit means being taken by God as His child and wrapped in His Love. In Satan's confrontation with God concerning Job,

Satan accused God: "Have You not made a hedge around him, around his household, and around all that he has on every side? You have blessed the work of his hands, and his possessions have increased in the land" Job 1: 10 (New King James).

The hedge mentioned by Satan was not intended for Job alone. The sealing work of the Holy Spirit places this hedge around each of us. Nothing can touch us or our loved ones or our possessions that doesn't first go through the encirclement of God's love, and then only for our ultimate good: "And we know that **all things work together for good** to those that love God, to those who are called according to His purpose" Romans 8: 28.

Now the second gift: "Who (the Holy Spirit) is **the guarantee of our inheritance** until the redemption of the purchased possession, to the praise of His glory" Ephesians 1:14.

It is customary for a bank in dealing with someone without established credit to require a co-signer, one who can guarantee the loan. In my Covenant with Jesus, the place for Him to sign is autographed in His own blood. Where I sign, two spaces are provided, one for me, and one for the Holy Spirit. He is the Co-Signer of my heavenly note, guaranteeing my salvation. It is imperative that we teach our children to understand the guidance of the Holy Spirit and to depend on it implicitly. The final text on the list describing the Holy Spirit's communication is: Brings us the constant assurance of our salvation. 1 John 3: 24

The word "assurance" referred to above will be greatly expanded on shortly.

So many times in my classes I have been asked by students my opinion on peripheral issues not explicitly touched on in God's law. You know these topics: movies, music, dress, jewelry, etc. When asked such questions, before any comment, I want to aid the questioners in identifying themselves. I reply, "Do you ask this from the standpoint of being a Christian or a non-Christian?" I then explain that if the question is asked from a non-Christian viewpoint, it doesn't really make any difference. I would suggest that life in this condition be so structured that there is no trouble with the law of our land; it's no fun in prison. Health should be maintained in order to have long life; for the non-Christian this life is all there is. On the other hand, as our children mature, they must learn that the ultimate guide to the Christian in such matters is not mom, dad, pastor, Bible teacher or any other human institution. Certainly, we would take time to discuss the pro's and con's of the situation, but Christians must find the answer based on their personal relationship with Jesus. That's why Christians are given knees! Yes, the home must have standards and the church as well, but there must come a time in the child's instruction when it is realized that the way Home is not determined by legislated goodness. Faith in

Jesus and trust in the Holy Spirit's guidance must combine in the soul of the believer in order to find the way Home.

THE COVENANT, Part Three: No Condemnation — JOHN 3:17,18

"For God did not send His Son into the world to condemn the world, but that the world through Him might be saved.

<u>He who believes in Him is not condemned; but he who does not believe is condemned already</u>, because he has not believed in the name of the only begotten Son of God."

Paul wrote:

"There is therefore now no condemnation to those who are in Christ Jesus, who do not walk according to the flesh, but according to the Spirit" Romans 8: 1.

Condemnation is a judgment term. A condemned person has been found guilty in some court of law. A few years ago a student came to me with a question: "Uncle Larry, you keep quoting Ephesians 2; 8-9: 'For by grace you have been saved through faith, and that not of yourselves; it is the gift of God.

Not of works, lest any one should boast.' (this text will be dealt with in more detail in a moment) But in every text I find in the Bible on the judgment it is emphasized that we are judged by our works. (He was a good student and had memorized everything I had assigned. To prove his point, he quoted 2 Corinthians 5: 10) ' For we must all appear before the judgment seat of Christ, that we may receive the things done in the body, according to what he has done, whether good or bad.' It seems to me that God is talking out of both sides of his mouth. In one place He says our works have nothing to do with our salvation, yet when He gets us in judgment He will judge us on our works."

This young man was an excellent student and had a very valid question . I directed his attention to another text he had memorized, Acts 3:19: "Repent therefore and be converted that your sins <u>may be blotted out</u>, so that times of refreshing may come from the presence of the Lord." I then explained this "blotting out" means there is nothing in the heavenly record of a Christian by which he could be condemned. Yes, our names come up in judgment. Yes, we are judged by our deeds but ,praise God, all sin is covered by the blood of Jesus! As Paul explains so well in his eighth chapter of Romans: "Who shall bring a charge against God's elect? It is God who justifies.

Who is he who condemns? It is Christ who died, and furthermore is also risen, who is even at the right hand of God, who also makes intercession for us" Romans 8: 33,34.

THE COVENANT, Part four: Jesus Changes Me — JOHN 3: 20,21

"For everyone practicing evil hates the light and does not come to the light, lest his deeds should be exposed. But he who does truth comes to the light, that his deeds may be clearly seen, that they have been done in God."

Here Jesus discusses our deeds or works. As a result of part 1, accepting Jesus, and part 2, the new birth, a change begins in my life. The closer I come to the Light, the more like Jesus I become. Recall Christ's words recorded in John, chapter fifteen:

"I am the true vine, My Father is the vine-dresser. Every branch in Me that does not bear fruit He takes away; and every branch that bears fruit He prunes, that it may bear more fruit" John 15:1, 2.

Notice the above verse carefully. If these were the only statements by Jesus on fruit bearing, our good works, we would be in real trouble. All of our lives would be spent in a frantic self-inspection to make sure we were doing enough good that the Father would not find it necessary to cut us off the vine. Talk about legalism! Praise God, Jesus didn't stop here. Notice the change in focus as He continued:

"You are already clean because of the word I have spoken to you. **Remain in Me and I will remain in you.** No branch can bear fruit by itself; **it must remain in the vine.** Neither can you bear fruit unless you remain in Me. I am the Vine; you are the branches. If a man remains in Me and I in him, he will bear much fruit; apart from Me you can do nothing. If anyone does not remain in Me, he is like a branch that is thrown away and withers; such branches are picked up, thrown into the fire and burned" John 15: 3-6 (NIV).

Now we see that our focus will never be on ourselves, but on the connection to the vine, Jesus. As long as we maintain that connection, we will always bear fruit. My brothers and sisters, **we can't stay with Jesus and stay the same**.

You see, there is a substance that flows through the vine that causes us as branches to be motivated to grow in Christ; to follow the lead of the Holy Spirit as we serve God and our fellow man. Paul identifies this substance: "The love of Christ compels us" II Corinthians 5:14 NKJ

This process may be called purification or sanctification; the terms are synonymous. In the second chapter of Titus, we found Jesus came to redeem and purify us. Part 1 of the covenant is redemption. Parts 2, 3 and 4 explain how sanctification is accomplished through the Holy Spirit.

All the New Testament authors base their teachings on the four principles Jesus taught Nicodemus.

Notice the words of Paul: "For by grace you have been saved through faith, and that not of yourselves, it is the gift of God, not of works, lest anyone should boast" (**Redemption**) Ephesians 2: 8,9.

"For we are His workmanship, created in Christ Jesus for good works, which God prepared beforehand that we should walk in them" (**Sanctification**) Ephesians 2: 10.

How does sanctification begin? "For this is the covenant I will make with the house of Israel after those days, says the Lord; I will put My laws in their mind, and write them in their hearts; and I will be to them a God, and they will be My people" Hebrews 8: 10.

(It must be kept in mind that Israel has always been God's name for the saved). Paul took a lot of time in his writings to explain this and to emphasize that the term, Israel, refers to Jew or Gentile in Christ (Romans 9:6-13; Galatians 3:27-29; Romans 11:26). This writing of God's law in my heart begins the instructional phase of the sanctification process. Notice how John explains this in his first epistle and does so in reference to the overall themes of redemption and purification: "Behold, what manner of love the Father has bestowed upon us that we should be called the sons of God: therefore the world doesn't know us, because it didn't know Him" **(Redemption)** 1 John 3:1.

"And everyone who has this hope in Him, purifies himself just as He is pure" **(Sanctification)** 1 John 3:3.

Next, John brings in the correlation between sanctification and God's law: "Whoever commits sin, also transgresses the law: for **sin is transgression of the law**" 1 John 3:4.

It is impossible for God to remove sin from my life if I don't know what sin is. His law gives this essential knowledge. Now, set this thought aside for a moment.

John's first letter seems to be a commentary on the third chapter of his gospel. The themes Jesus taught Nicodemus are taken by John and expanded into the best explanation of the Covenant in existence. John's purpose for writing this letter is found in 1 John 5: 13: "These things I have written to you who believe in the name of the Son of God, **that you may know you have eternal life,** and that you may continue to believe in the name of the Son of God."

I was introduced to the above text by a Baptist minister explaining his belief in what was once referred to as "once saved always saved." My problem with this concept, of course, was found in the tenth chapter of Hebrews which explains so clearly that if one gives up Jesus salvation is lost as well. But when I read the words, **these things have I written...that you may know,** my Adventist trained mind immediately asked, what things? For the first time I really read John's first letter, and it was as if the **these things** shone on the pages more brilliantly than any diamond. The book of First John was written to establish confidence, absolute assurance of our salvation! John explains **the five ways we can know we are saved.**

I. WALK IN THE LIGHT - I JOHN 1: 6, 7

"If we say that we have fellowship with Him and walk in darkness, we lie and do not practice the truth. But if we **walk in the light,** as He is in the light, we have fellowship with one another, and the blood of Jesus Christ His Son cleanses us from all sin."

Paul called this a "walk… after the Spirit" (Romans 8: 4). Jesus referred to it as abiding in Him (John 15: 1-6). It means communication in companionship, as if you were walking with a friend. Our abiding walk with Jesus, the Light, is based on prayer, the Word in Scripture, and meditation, giving God a chance to communicate back. If I fail to walk with Him, the danger is not that He will cast me out of His kingdom, but that I will cast away the Covenant. Jesus promised: "All that the Father gives Me will come to Me, and the one who comes to Me **I will by no means cast out"** John 6: 37.

When I taught this to students, the question always arose, "How can I know I'm walking in the light?"

I responded to this with a question of my own, "When was the last time you opened your heart to God as to a Friend?" I then explained I'm referring to taking the time to share with Him our plans and desires; to ask for His guidance; to allow Him the opportunity to point out areas of our lives which endanger the joy of the Covenant; to bestow grace as He forgives our sins. Was this today? Yesterday? Last week? Last month? Last year? If in answering these questions, we find we are dealing with long periods of time, it doesn't necessarily mean we're headed for hell, but it does mean we're working on it! To reverse this direction only takes a moment. We must always keep in mind that when Jesus returns, He is coming for His friends.

II. CONFESSION OF SIN -- 1 JOHN 1:9

"If we confess our sins, He is faithful and just to forgive us our sins, and to cleanse us from all unrighteousness."

When our conscience is convicted of wrong by the Spirit, we ask God to forgive our sin in the name of Jesus. As Jesus explained to His disciples, there is no limit to the number of times forgiveness is granted the sinner (Matthew 18:20, 21). All of us have weaknesses in our characters that cause us to fall so often. We must constantly keep in mind the promise of Jesus that if the branch will just stay connected to the Vine, fruit will appear, and our lives will change. That inner Power of the new birth constantly works to reproduce the character of Jesus in us. Never become discouraged, as will be amply verified in the next chapter. Jesus will never give up on us. This means there is hope for the weakest sinner that ever lived, even one as weak as I! This seems to cause trouble among some theologians who hold the view that before Jesus returns there must be people who have reached a sinless state of sanctification. I am no theologian, but there are two irrefutable Covenant promises that will determine this issue. One has been quoted previously: "All that the Father gives Me will come to me, and **whoever comes to Me I will never drive away.** For I have come down from heaven, not to do My will but to do the will of Him who sent Me. And this is the will of Him who sent Me, **that I shall lose none of all that He has given Me, but raise them up at the last day. For My Father's will is that everyone who looks to the Son and believes in Him shall have eternal life, and I will raise him up at the last day"** John 6: 37-40 (NIV).

The second: **"...I am with you always, even to the end of the age"** Matthew 28:20.

Confession must be preceded by repentance, sorrow for sin, and the sincere desire for Christ's power to overcome. If this repentance involves wrong to another person, it must be made right: "Confess your faults one to another and pray for one another, that you may be healed" James 5:16.

III. KEEP HIS COMMANDMENTS -- I JOHN 2: 3, 4

"Now by this we know that we know Him, **if we keep His commandments.** He who says, 'I know Him,' and doesn't keep His commandments **is a liar, and the truth is not in him."**

The thought you were asked to set aside a moment ago needs to be brought back, front and center. Sanctification begins with the writing of God's law in my heart. As can be seen by the clarity of John's statement above, if I don't keep the commandments, I am not saved. Paul expressed the same concept in these words:

"Because the carnal mind is enmity against God,

for it is not subject to the law of God, nor indeed can it be" Romans 8:7.

Both John and Paul based their thoughts about God's law on the encounter between Jesus and the rich young man recorded in Matthew 19:16-22: "Now behold, one came to Him and asked, 'Good teacher, what good thing shall I do that I may have eternal life?' And He said to him... 'If you will enter life, **keep the commandments.'** He said to Him, 'Which ones?' Jesus said, 'You shall not murder, you shall not commit adultery, you shall not steal, you shall not bear false witness, honor your father and mother, and, you shall love your neighbor as yourself.' "

But what is "keeping" the commandments? So much of what we as Seventh-day Adventists believe hinges on this, but far too many don't understand the meaning of the word "keep". To "keep" means to guard something precious, to treasure it. Keeping the commandments simply means you have allowed God to do what He promised, to write them in your heart, and you choose to live by those ten precepts. **You treasure and guard them as something precious.** It doesn't mean you are perfect now, or will be perfect in the future. In fact, the only thing keeping the commandments has to do with perfection is to point you in the direction of God's will. With all our hang-ups, frustrations, and tendencies for evil, we choose to follow that Will.

However, it does mean when we are convicted of

sin, we acknowledge the fact by repentance and confession. You see, because you and I have broken God's law, the blood of the Lamb of God had to be shed for us. We keep those commandments now because keeping goes beyond obedience to the foundation of obedience, love.

Have you ever by a careless word or action hurt someone you loved? Do you remember the heartache you felt when you realized what you had done? In just this way a person can be a commandment keeper and, yet, a commandment breaker. My brothers and sisters, we all find ourselves in this condition far too often. Then how can we tell who is saved or lost if both saved and lost are commandment breakers? The new Covenant Christian who breaks God's law realizes, through the influence of the Holy Spirit, the love relationship with Jesus has been violated, confesses, and is forgiven. Others who do wrong may be convicted of that wrong just as those under the Covenant, but there is no confession and, therefore, no forgiveness. **ALWAYS REMEMBER, KEEPING THE COMMANDMENTS SIMPLY MEANS YOU HAVE CHOSEN TO LIVE GOD'S WAY.**

We don't "try" to keep God's law. Either we choose to live by it or we don't. In the same way, we can't "try" to be a Christian; either we have accepted God's grace or we haven't. Certainly we "try" to be Christ-like as that inner Power of the new birth works in us. To ever state we try to be a Christian indicates there was an attempt to accept Christ, but somehow we never made it. When you accepted Jesus, you made it. Remember, Jesus promised if you stay with Him, you will continue to make it. Again: "For by grace you have been saved through faith, and that not of yourselves, it is the gift of God, not of works, lest anyone should boast."

Our salvation will never be **performance** based, but will always be **gift** based.

God's law is a unit. The Christian has no right to pick and choose which of the ten he wishes to keep and which he doesn't: "For whoever shall keep the whole law, and yet stumble in one point, he is guilty of all. For He who said, 'do not commit adultery,' also said, 'do not murder.' Now if you do not commit adultery, but you do murder, you have become a transgressor of the law. So speak and so do as those who will be judged by the law of liberty" James 2:10-12.

As we shall see, the third way we know we are saved is also the Third Angel's Message.

IV. LOVE OTHERS -- I JOHN 2: 9, 10

"He that says he is in the light, and hates his brother is in darkness until now. He who loves his brother abides in the light and there is no cause for stumbling in him."

As discovered earlier, we don't even know how to pray. The Holy Spirit must take our prayers and interpret them to the Father (Romans 8:26,27). The danger is the Holy Spirit doesn't interpret the prayer of our lips, but the prayer of our hearts. If I am asking forgiveness for myself but refuse to forgive my brother, my petition must be canceled. The Spirit has read the prayer of my heart! It doesn't matter how we or those close to us have been treated by others. It is so easy to find reasons to hate, but the Master demands: "But I say to you, **love your enemies,** bless those who curse you, do good to those who hate you, and pray for those who spitefully use you and persecute you" Matthew 5: 44.

There is absolutely no exemption from this command for the Christian. We love Jesus only as much as that one individual we despise the most: "Inasmuch as you did it to the least of these My brethren, you did it to Me" (Matthew 25: 40).

V. TO FIND OUT HOW IT IS BETWEEN ME AND JESUS, ALL I NEED TO DO IS ASK -- I JOHN 3:18-21

Earlier, Jesus introduced the new birth in the third chapter of John's gospel. Scripture texts were recorded illustrating the Holy Spirit's direct communication with the conscience. Keep this direct communication in mind as the following verses are carefully reviewed:

"My little children, let us not love in word, or in tongue, but in deed and in truth. And by this we know that we are of the truth, and shall assure our hearts before Him, For if our hearts condemn us, God is greater than our heart and knows all things.

Beloved, **if our hearts don't condemn us, we have confidence toward God."**

We have access to our heavenly record at any time. **It is impossible to overemphasize this largely overlooked provision in God's Covenant!!** The Holy Spirit uses our conscience to guarantee the assurance of our salvation. It is only necessary to ask the Father if there is anything in our lives endangering our Covenant relationship. If there is, He will convict us of it, bring to our mind the problem, giving us the opportunity of confession and forgiveness. "Now he who keeps His commandments abides in Him, and He in him. **And by this we know He abides in us, by the Spirit whom He has given us"** I John 3:24.

I have been asked many times if there is not some time in the future when the ministry of the Holy Spirit, outlined in this chapter, will be denied us. This question will be taken up in detail later. But for now I would emphasize that however this question is addressed it better be based on two rock-solid Covenant promises of Jesus: "… Lo, I am with you always, even to the end of the world". And … "For He Himself has said, ' I will never leave you nor forsake you ' Hebrews 13:5. Just as a bonus I would like to add one more Covenant promise: "All that the Father gives Me will come to Me, and the one who comes to Me **I will by no means cast out.** … This is the will of the Father who sent Me., that of all He has given Me **I should lose nothing, but should raise it up at**

the last day. John 6: 37,39.

I am constantly amazed at the determination of so many Seventh-Day Adventists to find some way to doubt! To many, the very thought that we know we are saved is presumptuous. These poor souls are determined to wander through life, hoping against hope that maybe they are saved. Sadly, the basis of this attitude is fear and denies a major covenant promise, one that will be used again later:

"For God has not given us a spirit of fear, **but of power and of love and of sound mind.**" II Timothy 1: 7

Shortly before Paul died, he penned his final testimony of victory by God's grace: "…. The time of my departure is at hand. I have fought the good fight, I have finished the race, I have kept the faith. Finally, there is laid up for me the crown of righteousness, which the Lord, the righteous Judge, will give to me on that day, **and not to me only, but to all who love His appearing**" II Timothy 4: 6-8.

Notice, there is absolutely no doubt in this statement. To harbor the thought that this confidence was in some way only for Paul or Peter or John destroys not only what they were trying to teach us but everything Jesus taught as well. My Adventist brother or sister, the Gospel can never coexist with doubt! The power of the Holy Spirit is severely limited in such an atmosphere. Paul meant every syllable when he commanded, "Let us come boldly to the throne of grace, that we may obtain mercy and find grace to help in time of need"

(Hebrews 4:16).

There is much in present day Adventist literature emphasizing the need to prepare our characters in preparation for the cataclysmic events soon to take place preceding Christ's return. This is certainly appropriate. However, I would submit that the greatest preparation better be the removal of any and all doubt concerning our salvation. The main purpose of the Covenant is to remove that doubt and to explain unequivocally **that our salvation will always be gift based, never performance based.**

The basics of Christ's Covenant with His people have been covered. He signed this agreement with His own blood. As Jesus explained on the occasion we call the Last Supper: "And as they were eating, Jesus took bread, blessed it and broke it, and gave it to the disciples and said, 'Take, eat; this My body.' Then He took the cup, and gave thanks, and gave it to them, saying, 'Drink from it, all of you. For this is My blood of the new covenant, which is shed for many for the remission of sins' " Matthew 26:26-28.

It was the Covenant that Paul and the other apostles carried "house to house," turning the world upside down. It will do so again.

Now, for a spiritual reality check.

1. Walk in the Light – Is Jesus your companion and confidant?

2. Confess your sins – When convicted of sin by the

Holy Spirit, do you ask forgiveness for that which He indicates is wrong?

3. Keep the commandments – Have you chosen to follow God's will?

4. Love others – Have you allowed hatred in any way to become part of your reality?   If so, are you willing to let Jesus have it?

5. Remember, you have access to your heavenly record at any time. Your salvation need never be in doubt.

Chapter Eight

Abraham And The Covenant

The best illustration of the Covenant relationship between God and man is found in the life of Abraham. The writer of Hebrews records this life in these words:

> "By faith Abraham obeyed when he was called to go out to the place he would afterward receive as an inheritance. And he went out, not knowing where he was going. By faith he sojourned in the land of promise as in a foreign country, dwelling in tents with Isaac and Jacob, heirs with him of the same promise; for he waited for a city which has foundations, whose builder and maker is God. By faith Sarah herself received strength to conceive seed, and she bore a child when she was past the age, because she judged Him faithful who had promised" Hebrews 11: 8-11.

No wonder God loved Abraham and Sarah

so much. They had such faith they never had the problems the rest of us have! Something is missing in the account above. In order for us to find this missing element, it will be necessary to compare the record in Hebrews with the one in Genesis.

God offered the same Covenant to Abraham He offers to us today. Abraham was to follow the Lord.

"Now the Lord said to Abram: "Get out of your country, from your kindred and from your father's house, to a land I will show you. **And I will make you a great nation"** Genesis 12: 1,2.

"I will make". This is the same promise given through Paul, "For we are His workmanship, created in Christ Jesus for good works" Ephesians 2: 10.

But Abram was so human: the spirit was willing, the flesh weak. Abram, father of the faithful, God's ambassador to the heathen, became fearful as he traveled to Egypt and denied his trust in the covenant:

"And it came to pass, when he was close to entering Egypt, that he said to Sarai, his wife. . . Say you are my sister, that it may be well with me for your sake" Genesis 12:11-13.

Sure enough, Pharoah was so impressed with Sarai he

took her. It wasn't until God plagued the Egyptains that she was returned to Abram. Pharoah was certainly made aware of Abram's God, but God's special ambassador was hustled out of Egypt in disgrace.

Years after Abram returned to Canaan, a dispute arose between Abram and his nephew, Lot, concerning pasture for their herds. After their painful separation, God came to Abram again and reaffirmed the covenant:

> "And the Lord said to Abram after Lot had
> Separated from him: "Lift your eyes now and look
> From the place where you are – northward,
> southward, eastward, and westward. For all the
> land which you see, I give to you and your
> descendants forever. . .Arise, walk in the land
> through its length and its width, for I give it to
> you" Genesis 13:14-17.

Years passed and still Abram had no son. Frustration had built to the point that Abram was convinced it would be necessary for him to help God keep His promise. The Lord returned in vision to give encouragement:

> "After these things the word of the Lord came to
> Abram in a vision, saying, "Do not be afraid, Abram
> I am your shield, your exceedingly great reward."

Abram hardly paid attention; he had heard all this before. He was ready to offer a solution:

> "But Abram said, 'Lord God what will you give

me, seeing I go childless, and the heir of my house is Eliezer of Damascus. Then Abram said, Look, You have given me no offspring; indeed, one born in my house is my heir!"

Patiently God rejected Eliezer, explaining the child of promise would come from Abram's body, and then He repeated the terms of the covenant:

"Then He brought him outside and said, "Look now toward heaven, and count the stars if you are able to number them." And He said to him, "So shall your descendant be. And he believed in the Lord; and **He counted it to him as righteousness"** Genesis 15:1-6.

For the first time in Scripture it was explained that our faith, as weak as it may be, is placed on our heavenly account and justifies us in God's sight. "The just shall live by faith" Romans 1:17.

More years pass, still no child. Now Sarai enters the picture, blames the problem on God, and suggests her solution:

"So Sarai said to Abram, 'See now, the Lord has restrained me from bearing children. Please go in to my maid; perhaps I shall obtain children by her.' And Abram heeded the voice of Sarai. . . he went Into Hagar and she conceived" Genesis 16:1-4.

The trap Satan laid for Abram and Sarai in this

experience would not only threaten their relationship (Genesis 16:5,6), but cause untold hardship. Ishmael, Abram's son by Hagar, became an outcast from Abram's home and later fathered the Arab race. Eventually, God's promise would be fulfilled. Abram and Sarai's son, Isaac, would father the Jewish race (Genesis 29:1-4). The hatred between Arab and Jew engendered by this experience has lasted for thousands of years and is a major item practically on a daily basis in news headlines today.

God's tenacity, His refusal to give up on us, demonstrated in His treatment of Abram is beyond belief. After the debacle over Hagar, the Lord once again returned with the covenant promise:

> "When Abram was ninety-nine years old, the Lord
> Appeared to Abram and said to him, 'I am
> Almighty God; walk before Me and be blameless.'
> And I will make My covenant between Me and
> you. . . you shall be a father of many nations"
> Genesis 17:1-4.

God's continuing instruction to Abraham (the name change is found in Genesis 17:5) reveals one of the most amazing exchanges ever recorded:

> "Then God said to Abraham, 'As for Sarai, your
> wife, you shall not call her Sarai, but Sarah shall be
> her name.' And I shall bless her and also give you a
> son by her. . . she shall be a mother of nations;

kings of people shall be from her."

At this juncture Abraham couldn't take it anymore. He had been hearing this for twenty-four years, and his faith was in tatters!

> "Then Abraham fell on his face and laughed and
> said in his heart, 'Shall a child be born to a man who
> is one hundred years old? And shall Sarah, who is
> ninety years old, bear a child?"

By this time Abraham was on a roll and out of control! You can almost hear the anguish in his voice as we read his words:

> "And Abraham said to God, ' Oh, that Ishmael
> Might live before You!' "

Laughed at God? Begged Him to accept his way? With infinite patience the Lord answered a man who loved Him, but just couldn't understand:

> "Then God said, 'No, Sarah your wife shall bear
> You a son, and you shall call his name Isaac' "
> Genesis 17:15-19.

Later, as the Lord and two angels were on their way to Sodom and Gomorrah to render judgment, they stopped by Abraham's encampment:

> "Then they said to him, 'Where is Sarah your wife?'
> And he said, 'Here in the tent.' And He said, 'I will
> Certainly return to you according to the time of life,
> and, behold, Sarah your wife shall have a son.'

And Sarah was listening in the tent door which was behind Him. . . Sarah laughed with in herself, saying, "After I have grown old, shall I have pleasure, my Lord being old also?" And the Lord said to Abraham, "Why did Sarah laugh, saying, 'Shall I Surely bear a child, now that I am old?' Is anything Too hard for the Lord? At the appointed time I will Return to you, according to the time of life, and Sarah shall have a son." But Sarah denied it, saying, "I did not laugh," for she was afraid. And he said, "No, but you did laugh" Genesis 18:9-15.

Laughed at God? Lied to Him? As if this weren't bad enough, notice what happened when they were given the opportunity to witness before another king:

"And Abraham journeyed from there to the south . . . Now Abraham said of Sarah his wife, 'She is my sister.' And Abimelech, king of Gerar, sent And took Sarah."

The Lord came to the rescue and bailed this pair out again:

"But God came to Abimelech in a dream by night, and said, 'Indeed you are a dead man because of the woman you have taken, for she is a man's wife."

The Lord certainly had Abimelech's attention! After Abeimelech's proclamation of innocence, God gave him these directions:

"Now restore the man's wife, **for he is a prophet,**

And he will pray for you, and you shall live. But if

You do not restore her, know that you shall die,

and all that are yours" Genesis 20:1-7.

A prophet? At this point, if you or I had been in charge, there would have been many words used to describe Abraham, but "prophet" wouldn't be among them! Certainly, now would be a good time to just let these two go their way, leave them alone, and find someone else who would really appreciate the covenant. Praise the Lord, we're not in charge! How is God, the Ruler of the universe, going to handle this faithless demonstration?

"And the Lord visited Sarah as He had said, and the

Lord did for Sarah as He had spoken. For Sarah

conceived and bore Abraham a son in his old age, at

the set time of which God had spoken to him Amd

Abraham called the name of his son. . . Issac"

Genesis 21:1-3.

It's easy to see why God gave this pair a son. They had demonstrated such steadfast confidence in God's promise He rewarded them with a boy, right? Wrong!? Well, let's try this. Abraham and Sarah were such excellent ambassadors before the kings the Lord sent them to that He gave them a child. What!? Wrong again!? Well, we're running out of options, but let's try this. God kept His promise and gave them Isaac. We finally got it? Reader, our promise of salvation is exactly the same! Allow me to repeat just once more, "For by grace you are saved through faith, and that not of yourselves, it is the gift of God" Ephesians 2:8.

Rather than being a whitewashed fabrication, Genesis faithfully records the failures as well as the victories of Abraham and Sarah. We can certainly relate to them since we see ourselves mirrored in their struggle with faith and sin. But wait a minute! In the beginning of this chapter, we found the writer of Hebrews praising this pair to high heaven. He was surely better acquainted with the Genesis account than we are.   It's time we discovered the missing element that makes the accounts of both Genesis and Hebrews accurate. We must begin in the book of Acts:

> "Repent therefore and be converted. **That your sins may be blotted out,** that times of refreshing may come from the presence of the Lord" Acts 3:19.

Under the crushing load of remorse and guilt suffered by David after the prophet Nathan condemned him for adultery with Bathsheba and the murder of Uriah, David penned these words:

> "Have mercy upon me, O God, According to your Loving kindness; According to the multitude of Your tender mercies, **Blot out my transgressions. . . .** Hide your face from my sin, and **Blot out all my iniquities. . . create in me a clean heart, O God,** and renew a right spirit within me. Restore to me the joy of your salvation. . ." Psalms 51:1-12.

Our merciful Heavenly Father granted this poor sinner's request. You see, we call the eleventh chapter of Hebrews the "faith chapter." Faith is defined at the beginning (Hebrews 11:1), and the lives of saved individuals are recorded **as a result of faith. All sin is blotted out!** Reading Hebrews alone would give the impression Abraham and Sarah never sinned. **That is exactly the point! Only the good remains on their records. Talk about marvelous! Our records are doctored by Jesus in just the same way!** Our lack of faith, sin, whimpering, are all erased by the blood of the Savior.

~ Chapter Nine ~

The Covenant And The Most Terrible Warning In Scripture

(Revelation 14: 9-11)

I have tried to record on these pages the power I have witnessed in our message and especially the effect of this power on our youth. The Latter Rain outpouring of the Holy Spirit this church has longed for and prayed for, and the Third Angel's Message are one and the same. This chapter is an attempt to explain why this is true. I will warn you ahead of time: the study you are about to begin contains no surface material. It will take you as deep as you have ever been in Scripture. Ask the Holy Spirit to be your guide before you start.

In the fourteenth chapter of Revelation, there are three descriptions: the 144,000 (verses 1-5). The Three Angels' Messages (verses 6-14), and the return of Jesus (verses 15-20). Just reflecting on these three descriptions alone raises some intriguing questions: If the Three Angels' messages are not given, does Jesus return? If the 144,000, whoever they are,

are not formed, does history find its climax? These questions alone outline in lightning the awesome responsibility of the Seventh-day Adventist church. We are the only organization on Planet Earth solely dedicated to revealing from Scripture the meaning of God's last call to the human race. If you are looking for proof that our teachings inculcate the concept of God's remnant people, you need look no further than this fact. Understanding the Third Angel's Message is the key to the power promised us as a people: "Then a third angel followed them, saying with a loud voice, 'If anyone worships the beast and his image, and receives his mark on his forehead or on his hand, he himself shall drink of the wine of the wrath of God, which is poured out full strength into the cup of His indignation'" Revelation 14:9, 10.

The Third Angel's Message is the strongest warning in Scripture. It would not be right for God to give a warning such as this and not provide a **clear** and **unmistakable** explanation. God is right, and, as we will see, His explanation in Scripture is both **clear** and **unmistakable.** As can be easily discerned from the above texts, we know the lost receive a mark on the forehead and hand. Oddly enough, a similar seal or mark is found on the foreheads of the saved: "Then I saw another angel ascending from the east, having a seal of the living God. And he cried with a loud voice to the four angels to whom it was granted to harm the earth and the sea, do not harm the earth, the sea, or the trees until we have sealed the servants of our God on their foreheads" Revelation 7:2, 3.

If both saved and lost receive the same symbol, what could it mean? To begin finding an answer, we must return to the experience of Israel being delivered from Egypt. On the night of that delivery, later to be called Passover, God gave the following instruction: "It (observing Passover) shall be as a sign to you on your hand and as a memorial between your eyes (the forehead) that **the Lord's law** may be in your mouth; for with a strong hand the Lord has brought you out of Egypt" Exodus 13:9.

Notice the correlation in the above text between the sign on the forehead and hand and God's law. In Deuteronomy, chapter five, verses 6-22, Moses records the ten Commandments just as they are in Exodus, chapter twenty. The next chapter (Deuteronomy, chapter six) is devoted to the instruction by Moses on these commandments. In those instructions we find these words: "You shall bind them (the Ten Commandments) as a **sign on your hand** and as frontlets **between your eyes** (the forehead)" Exodus 6:8.

Israel was not a nation until they left Egypt. The sign on the forehead and hand is the first symbol God used to denote His special people. It is both **clear** and **unmistakable** that in every instance in the Old Testament where a sign on the forehead and hand is used, it means allegiance to God expressed through keeping his Commandments. **It is the message of the Third Angel of Revelation, chapter fourteen,**

that brings this concept over to the New Testament.
The five ways we know we are saved were discovered in
John's first epistle. You will recall the third of those five is
keeping the commandments (1 John 2:3,4). Much time was
taken to explain that the word, "keep," means to treasure or
guard something precious; that keeping the commandments
means you have allowed God to write them in your heart,
and you choose to live by those principles. John went so far
as to say if we profess to follow Jesus and don't keep His
commandments, we are liars. **The Third Angel's Message
is a big, red warning sign with flashing lights held up in
Revelation saying:**

!! DANGER !!

!! DANGER !!

STOP: MAKE SURE YOU UNDERSTAND

THE TERMS OF THE COVENANT BEFORE

IT IS TOO LATE

**The only reason for the existence of the Seventh-
day Adventist Church is to hold up that sign!** The concept
is extremely simple: if we keep God's commandments, we
receive His mark or sign on the forehead (Revelation, chapter
seven, verses two and three); if you follow the commandments
of the beast, you receive the mark of that power on our
forehead and hand (Revelation, chapter fourteen, verses nine
and ten). Paul explained the basic principle behind the Third

Angel's Message in these words: "Do you not know that to whom you present yourselves slaves to obey, you are that one's slaves whom you obey, whether of sin to death, or of obedience to righteousness" Romans 6:16.

God doesn't just leave it here; in His Word He becomes extremely specific. He is determined there will be no room for misunderstanding exactly what He means. Notice what Isaiah said would take place while God's people waited for the Lord's return: "Bind up the testimony, **seal the law among My disciples**. And I will wait on the Lord, that hides His face from the house of Jacob, and I will look for Him" Isaiah 8: 16,17.

Although the Ten Commandments are a unit and to break one is to break them all (James 2:10-12), the Lord points directly at the fourth commandment as the special sign, seal, or mark of the Covenant relationship with His people. Jesus makes it crystal clear it is Sabbath power that correlates the three descriptions found in the fourteenth chapter of Revelation. **Christ documented this himself by his example and teaching recorded in the New Testament**. However, He carefully laid the foundation for this in the Old Testament.

First: the Sabbath is the sign between God and His people that He is Lord and Master. "Hallow My Sabbaths, **and they will be a sign between me and you, that you may know I am the Lord your God**" Ezekiel 20:20.

Second: the Sabbath is the sign between God and his people that He is Creator. "Therefore the children of Israel shall keep the Sabbath, to observe the Sabbath throughout their generations as a perpetual covenant. It is a sign between Me and the children of Israel forever; **for in six days the Lord made the heavens and the earth**, and on the seventh day He rested and was refreshed" Exodus 31: 16,17. (Keep in mind that Israel today is the Christian" Galatians 3: 26-29.)

Third: the Sabbath is the sign between God and His people that He is Sanctifier. "Speak also to the children of Israel, saying: 'Surely My Sabbaths you shall keep, for it is a sign between Me and you throughout your generations, **that you may know that I am the Lord who sanctifies you**" Exodus 31:13.

As will be seen, the sanctifying power of the Sabbath is a theme that runs deeply through Scripture from Genesis to Revelation. In order to even begin to understand this, we must return to the Sabbath's origin: "And on the seventh day God ended His work which He had done, and He **rested** on the seventh day from all the work which He had done. Then God **blessed** the seventh day and **sanctified** it" Genesis 2:2,3.

The concept of rest in these verses is not physical rest. Sabbath rest is much more comprehensive and includes the blessing of sanctification. Jesus put all this together for us in the gospel record. Isaiah, the gospel prophet, predicted what

Christ would do with God's law: "The Lord is well pleased for His righteousness sake. He will **magnify the law** and make it honorable" Isaiah 42:21.

It goes without saying, we magnify something to make it larger, enabling us to see it better. A segment of Christ's message we call the Sermon on the Mount was devoted to His concept of the law of God. He began that explanation with these words:

"Do not think that I came to destroy the law and the prophets. I did not come to destroy but to fulfill. For assuredly, I say to you, till heaven and earth pass away, one jot or one tittle shall by no means pass away till all is fulfilled" Matthew 5:17,18.

As Jesus continued, He began fulfilling Isaiah's prophecy by magnifying, or making clearer, the law. First, the sixth commandment: "You have heard it was said to those of old, 'You shall not murder, and whoever murders shall be in danger of the judgment.' But I say to you that whoever is angry with his brother without a cause shall be in danger of the judgment" Matthew 5:21,22.

Since Jesus spoke these words, the world has understood the sixth commandment not only invokes us against killing, but hatred as well. Next, He did the same for the seventh commandment: "You have heard it was said to those of old, 'You shall not commit adultery.' But I say to you that whoever looks at a woman to lust for her has already committed adultery with her in his heart" Matthew 5: 27,28.

Christ didn't magnify all ten of the commandments in this sermon. Over the next three and one half years, he would find opportunity to clarify the other eight. In the eleventh and twelfth chapters of Matthew, He magnified the Sabbath. Jesus was taking a Sabbath walk (Matthew 12:1) when He said: "Come to me, all you who labor and are heavy laden and I will give you rest. Take my yoke upon you and learn from Me, for I am gentle and lowly in heart, and you will find **rest for your souls**. For My yoke is easy and my burden is light" Matthew 11: 28-30.

"Soul rest" is allowing the Holy Spirit to combine the Creator's Sabbath blessing of sanctification with that inner power of the new birth. It is a weekly appointment with Jesus for a soul-check. Recall that Jesus said the purpose of the Commandments was to bring us "full joy" (John 15:10,11). This must be the foundation of our approach to the soul rest of Sabbath observance. The day is to be a celebration of our Covenant and filled with joy.

As Jesus continued that Sabbath walk with his friends, He began magnifying the Sabbath by removing the bondage and misunderstanding the Jews had strapped on the day. It didn't take long for a conflict to develop with the Pharisees: "At that time Jesus went through the grain fields on the Sabbath and His disciples were hungry, and began to pluck heads of grain and to eat. But when the Pharisees saw it, they said to Him, "Look, Your disciples are doing what is not lawful on the Sabbath"

Matthew 12:1,2.

In the next verses, Jesus explained that the promised Sabbath rest was based on a relationship with the "Lord of the Sabbath" (Matthew 12:8), rather than rules and regulations. Not satisfied, the Pharisees drew attention to a crippled man nearby and asked: "And behold, there was a man with a crippled hand. And they asked Him, saying, 'Is it lawful to heal on the Sabbath?'---that they might accuse Him. Then He said to them, 'What man is there among you that has one sheep, and if it falls into a pit on the Sabbath, will not lay hold of it and pull it out? Of how much more value then is a man than a sheep? **Therefore it is lawful to do good on the Sabbath.'** Then He said to the man, 'Stretch out your hand.' And he stretched it out, and it was restored as whole as the other. Then the Pharisees went out and held counsel against Him, **how they might destroy Him"** Matthew 12:10-14.

Now the world could understand that Sabbath soul rest included helping others: "It is lawful to do good on the Sabbath."

It is true there were many teachings of Jesus that upset the Jewish leadership. However, it was Christ's magnification of the Sabbath that pushed them over the brink of deciding to kill Him, a fact born out even more strongly by the gospel writer, Mark (Mark 2:23-28; Mark 3:6). The close correlation between Sabbath soul rest and sanctification represents a mortal threat to Satan's empire.

The 144,000 (keep in mind, this is the <u>name of this</u> group, not the actual number) are the living saved at Christ's return. In the description of them in the fourteenth chapter of Revelation, we find the Father's name is written on their foreheads (Revelation 14:1). As has been amply documented, that forehead symbol is only received by keeping the Commandments, including the Sabbath. Will they all be Seventh-day Adventists? Certainly not. Sabbath keepers? Certainly, yes. This is why in every description of God's last-day people, we find they "keep the commandments of God and have the faith of Jesus" (Rev. 14: 12, Rev. 12:17).

Scripture repeatedly emphasizes Satan will deceive the whole world (Rev. 12:9, Rev.13:3). The crowning act of that deception will be the counterfeit of Christ's return. Paul describes this in the second chapter of Thessalonians: "The coming of the lawless one is according to the working of Satan, **with all power, signs and lying wonders**" II Thessalonians 2:9.

The word, "coming," in verse nine is the Greek word, *parousia*, the same word used for Christ's "coming" at the Second Advent (II Thess. 2:1, Matt. 24:3), the only other use of the word in Scripture. (This *parousia* by Satan is described in <u>The Great Controversy</u>, pages, 593-625.) Paul next explains why so many will be deceived : "...and with all unrighteous deception among those who perish, **because they did not receive the love of the truth, that they might be saved**" II Thessalonians 2:10.

The testing truths of our message -- the Sabbath, the sleep of death, the way Christ returns -- are tailored to enable Christians to reject the false and wait for the True: "For false Christs and false prophets will arise and show great signs and wonders, **so as to deceive, if possible, even the elect**" Matthew 24:24.

This is the imperative of the third angel's message!

Sunday sacredness, the secret rapture, the dead don't die, and other falsehoods are tailored by Satan to prepare the world for his great act. Make no mistake: when he appears, the world will call his name, Jesus. I find the concept seeping into our midst that all those beautiful Christians around have found salvation in Jesus; therefore, we have no need for such urgency in reaching them with present truth. I can only hope a deeper understanding of the significance of the Third Angel's Message will quell this concept.

It is a truism that each person who has ever lived or will live on earth is unique. That means that each finite person represents an image of the Creator that will never exist in another. God doesn't necessarily see us as we are now, but as we will become in a thousand or billion years from now as our one-of-a-kind image of the Creator expands throughout eternity. My friend, you represent a jewel in God's creation that will never be reproduced. If God loses you, your unique image of Him is lost for eternity. As His children, God sees Himself in each of us. That's why He loves us so much, warts and all; why a man like David could be "a man after God's own heart"; or Abraham could be "a friend to God"; why He accepts each of us with only one condition, that we "walk in the Light"; why it is true Jesus would have given Himself for just one of us.

If we could only realize this! So many times in counseling young and old alike, we recognize the condition labeled, low self-esteem. Such a person sees himself as worth so little with small prospect of there ever being a change in circumstances for the better. Who? Who could ever care for them? The tragedy is they see themselves through Satan's eyes. In the eyes of Jesus, we are all children of the King, a one-of-a-kind representation of our Father.

Reader, this chapter might represent your first opportunity to be introduced to the 7th day Sabbath. If you wish to be sure of Christ's will concerning this topic, there is a simple solution. Read Exodus 20: 8-11, then on your knees ask in Jesus name to have the Holy Spirit clear your mind of preconceived ideas and prejudices. Now, ask Jesus if you should observe the Sabbath. Remember I John 3: 18-21?

~ Chapter Ten ~

I Think So, I Hope So

As we have seen, Jesus has made every effort to make
sure we know exactly where we stand with Him. There is no
excuse for doubt or fears concerning our salvation:

> "For God has not given us the spirit of fear, but of
> power and of love and of a sound mind"
> II Timothy 1:7.

Then why is it so many of my brothers and sisters in the
Seventh-day Adventist Church live in doubt and uncertainty?

So many times when I have presented the clear Word on
spiritual assurance I have seen a pulling back, followed by the
words, "But Sister White sez." Yes, it's true that many of her
statements taken at face value throw doubt on our assurance.

Here are a few:

"Those who accept the Savior, however sincere their
conversion, should never be taught to say or to feel that they
are saved" Christ's Object Lessons, p. 155.

"We are never to rest in a satisfied condition, and cease

to make advancement saying, 'I am saved' . . . No sanctified tongue will be found uttering these words till Christ comes. . .' He should never dare to say, 'I am saved'. " Selected Messages, Book One, p. 314.

The denomination has tried repeatedly to demonstrate that these quotations were a warning against the falsehood, "Once saved always saved." The best I personally have read explaining what Ellen White really meant by the quotations above was in Phillip Durham's book, SURE SALVATION. He not only takes up these troublesome quotes, but he documents numerous times Ellen White confirmed the absolute assurance of salvation.

Be that as it may, far too many Seventh-day Adventists have taken these statements at face value and the results have been devastating, not only to those in the church, but to those outside of our denomination as well. Millions of Seventh-day Adventists have gone to their graves never really trusting that Jesus had accepted them. At the present time millions more suffer the same doubt and confusion. How sad Jesus must be that not only His words of assurance, but the Holy Spirit's instruction in John's first letter that established point after point of that same confidence, even to direct access to our salvation record, seems to have been disregarded by so many.

A few years ago I was in a meeting that included a good friend, the ministerial secretary of a local conference. During the discussion my friend made a statement that concerned me. Later, I was with him and asked, "Bill, (not his name) do you know you are saved?"

His face took on an expression I have seen all too often. I knew what was coming and my heart sank. He answered, "I think so, I hope so."

I then asked, "On what basis do you 'think so, hope so'?"

There was a pause; then he returned, "Well, this morning I studied my Sabbath School lesson and had prayer."

I've heard this type of reply at every level of our church, General Conference to layman.

Joy is an integral concept in Christ's teaching. Here is another Covenant promise:

> "These things I have spoken to you, that My joy may remain in you, and that your joy might be full"
> John 15:11.

Let's check this out with a good Baptist believer:

"Sir, are you a Christian?"

He responds, "Why, yes, praise God."

"Do you find joy in your belief?, I continue. Before he can respond, tears rim just back of his eyelids. Emotion causes him to hesitate before he can answer: "Man, Jesus saved me. I had never known peace until I knew I was in God's kingdom. I rejoice every day I walk with Jesus!"

Now we approach our God-fearing, commandment-keeping, faithful- tithe-returning, "I think so, I hope so," Adventist believer. Again, I ask, "Sir are you a Christian?"

His answer, "Well, I certainly try to be." (We're in trouble already, but we forge ahead). "Does your belief bring you joy?"

"Yes, it does", he replies

"Why?" I continue.

"Maybe I'm saved," he answers.

There can be no true joy in maybe, in "I think so, I hope so."

Paul admonishes us: "Do not cast away your confidence, which has great reward" Hebrews 10:35.

This is no problem to our "I think so, I hope so" believers. The great tragedy is, it is impossible to throw away what one never possessed.

As a student in Adventist schools, I was taught religiously that I could never know I was saved, and, horror of horrors, must never say, "I am saved" (remember, this was **PRESUMPTION!**). And we were taught something called imparted righteousness, which was defined as, do the best you can and Jesus will make up the difference. That definition is anathemy to the Gospel. In actuality the righteousness of Christ is imparted to us at every step we take in our walk in the Light.

The old song says:

"Jesus paid it all. All to Him I owe. Sin had left a

crimson stain. He washed it white as snow."

Far too many have sung those words but were believing:

"Jesus paid a part. I'll pay part myself. Sin had left a crimson stain. We'll wash it white as snow."

No, the old song had it right. Jesus paid it all!

At the beginning of this chapter, it was stated that those misunderstood Ellen White writings not only were devastating within our church but outside as well.

I was in a discussion on Scripture with a believer of another faith when she asked what church I belonged to. I answered, "Seventh-day Adventist." Immediately her eyes took on the expression of the cat just before eating the canary. She asked, "Are you saved?" She waited expectantly for my answer. She had asked many Adventists this and thought she knew what I was about to answer. I said, "Praise God, yes! I rejoice every moment in the victory Jesus paid for me."

The look of chagrin that possessed her features was almost comical. But it was anything but funny.

The power of our witness has in far too many instances been destroyed by the answer, "I think so, I hope so."

In the second chapter as Maranatha was described, I mentioned the invitation given to a few of my students and me to visit Florida Bible College. We were invited also to attend their student assembly. Looking back, I believe we were invited to that school for the express purpose of that gathering of their faculty and students because during the presentation it was mentioned with sadness by the speaker his concern that so many Seventh-day Adventists were clueless as to whether or not they were saved.

Later I visited with this man, the academic dean of the college. He showed me his personal library and then took from the shelves several of Ellen White's books. He handed me his copy of <u>Steps To Christ</u> and asked that I leaf through it. The book was underlined with notations in the margins and cross referenced with Scripture. He knew our message but had been turned off by the few quotations discussed earlier.

There is nothing we can do about those who oppose our message and use our own writings against us. But this is not the case when it comes to our believers. In our pulpits and especially in our schools we must do a far better job of grounding our people in the Covenant promises of Jesus and especially John's five ways we know we are saved.

We must consider one other Covenant promise by Jesus:

"And this gospel of the kingdom will be preached in all the world as a witness to all nations, and then the end will come" Matthew 24:14.

Notice that Jesus gives only one prerequisite for His return: finish the gospel commission to "go and teach" (Matthew 28:19, 20).

Paul explained in Hebrews, chapter nine, that the life and teachings of Jesus were His last will and testament and that this testament was sealed by His blood (Hebrews 9:14).

Any codicil or change in His will must be made before His death and only by Jesus Himself since His will was to go into effect after His death (Hebrews 9:16, 17).

Many believe that Ellen White attempted to add a codicil to Christ's will in these words: "Christ is waiting with longing desire for the manifestation of Himself in His people. When the character of Christ shall be perfectly reproduced in His people, then He will come to claim them as His own" Christ's Object Lessons, p. 69.

In other words, Christ's promise to come after a completed gospel was not enough. We must become as perfect as He is; then He will return. Do we really believe that Ellen White had the audacity to believe she had the authority to make a codicil to a blood-sealed promise of Christ? I, for one don't believe that was her intention. Yet, so many in our church have taken these words and run right out and thrown the Bible under the bus!

I am amazed when I talk to those who hold the view of absolute perfection demanded by Jesus before He comes back. When asked about this, invariably their eyes take on the shine of the true believer as they explain we must show the universe we can do it too.

I ask, "Do what, too?"

The response, "Be just as perfect as Jesus was. You see, after probation closes the Holy Spirit not only is taken out of the world, but from us as well. We must become so good we can stand without a Mediator!"

My next question, "What about the Covenant promises of Jesus that He would be with us to the end (Matthew 26:20) and that He would never leave us nor forsake us (Hebrews 13:52)"?

After a long pause, "Well, I guess we will be so good we won't need them!"

Jesus warned us that the tribulation coming after probation's close will be the harshest God's people have ever faced (Matthew 24: 21). There will be a total world government (Revelation 17:13-18) that not only has denied any financial avenue of support to God's people (Revelation 13:17), but is determined to exterminate them (Revelation 13:5). There is no doubt that those who live through this time and "keep the commandments of God and the faith of Jesus"(Revelation 14: 12) will need the ministry, comfort and direction of the Holy Spirit more than at any time in history. Yet, so many Adventist believers are convinced God will deny this to them.

I can't understand what is going on with those who hold such views. Do they deny that Jesus promised to be with us to the end and never leave us nor forsake us? Do they believe He was lying and, therefore, can't be trusted? To believe that Jesus forsakes His people and refuses to honor his Covenant promise in the time of their greatest need, tinges on blasphemy and denial of the Savior! It would really be a good idea to carefully check all our teachings with Scripture!

If there is any apparent disparity, even to the slightest degree, between the writings of Ellen White and Scripture, it is Ellen White's work that must be re-examined and if need be adjusted, **never the Bible!** Does this mean I don't treasure Ellen White's work? Of course not.

Here is the crux of the matter. In order to complete the commission given to the Seventh-day Adventist Church in the Three Angel's Messages we must have the fulfillment of the blessings of the Latter Rain. If we think this power will be bestowed when so many of our people are confused about their salvation and earnestly believe concepts completely alien to the Covenant promises of Jesus, we are in for a long wait!!!

~ Chapter Eleven ~

The Task

The Scriptural clarity of the explanation of the Third Angel's Message brings home to all of us the responsibility of proclaiming God's last message to a dying planet. I know of no other religious group that gives a clear Biblical interpretation of the strongest warning ever given - Revelation 14:6-12. Instead I hear from supposedly Biblical scholars fanciful pronouncements: "The mark of the beast is 666!"; "There will be a computer chip placed in the hand and forehead!!"; "The Antichrist will demand an invisible tattoo to indicate allegiance!!!"

It is no wonder Ellen White penned the following admonition: "In a special sense, Seventh-day Adventist have been set in the world as watchmen and light bearers. To them has been entrusted the last warning for a perishing world. On them is shining wonderful light from the Word of God. They have been given a work of most solemn import – The proclamation of the first, second, and third angels' messages.

There is no other work of so great importance. They are to allow nothing else to absorb their attention" Testimonies For The Church, Vol. 9, p. 19.

And this: "The Third Angel's Message is the gospel message for these last days, and in no case is it to be overshadowed by other interests and made to appear an unessential consideration. **When in our institutions anything is placed above the Third Angel's Message, the gospel is not there the great leading power"** Testimonies For The Church, Vol. 6, p. 131.

It has been made clear to us our primary concern in accomplishing our task must be the training of our young people.

The most quoted statement concerning Adventist youth ever made by Ellen White is: "With such an army of workers as our youth, **rightly trained,** might furnish, how soon the message of a crucified, risen, and soon-coming Savior might be carried to the whole world! How soon might the end come – the end of suffering and sorrow and sin!" Education, p. 271.

I would like to make a few suggestions that might help us focus on this concept of "rightly trained":

1. A prerequisite for graduation from an Adventist academy or college should be to have a good Bible the student has personally marked with our message and be able to demonstrate they know how to use it.

2. A large portion of our youth never attend an Adventist school. A local church program should be developed designed to educate these young people in the responsibility of our message. They should be given the same opportunity to prepare a good Bible and know how to use it.

3. In our training institutions, future pastors and teachers should take classes together designed to train them to cooperate in youth evangelism.

4. There is a "window" in the lives of young people that represents the optimum time to learn evangelistic skills. For most, this is from late teenage years to the early twenties. This is the exact age range of the young religious revolutionaries that began the Advent movement. If evangelistic training is not provided during this time, the chances of an Adventist ever becoming involved in personal evangelism drops to four or five percent. Beyond this time the cares of life begin to dominate: job, family, payments, etc. This does not mean there is no interests; it just becomes increasingly difficult to find the time to learn.

And it takes time to learn soul-winning skills. None of us are born with this ability. With this in mind, we should develop a voluntary program that will allow young people in the above age range to take a year or more to go into the field to learn personal evangelism.

I am a Texan. Born in Grand Prairie (friend, that is not the forest capitol of the good old U.S. of A.) and raised among the rolling hills, valleys, lakes, streams and deep woods of East Texas. In the small schools I attended, there may have been gaps in our educational process, but Texas history wasn't one of them. Places like the Alamo and San Jacinto were sacred shrines that stood for honor, determination, courage, and self-sacrifice. We were made to feel that each one that died in the fight for Texas independence was like the loss of a personal friend or a family member. Every week our principal would take us outside to pledge allegiance to the flag; then he would lead us in singing what I thought surely was the National Anthem, The Eyes of Texas. I must admit, the state song of Texas certainly isn't very sophisticated, but the words convey love and acceptance, as well as a gut-level sense of responsibility. Now that I am a Christian, I've changed the lyrics a little:

> The eyes of Jesus are upon you,
> all the livelong day.
> The eyes of Jesus are upon you,
> you cannot get away.
> Do not think you can escape them
> from dawn till early in the morn.
> The eyes of Jesus are upon you
> till Gabriel blows his horn!"

* * *

Biography

Larry Stephens is an ordained minister who has enjoyed the honor of working for 36 of his 49 years of service with thousands of young people as a teacher and counselor. He is the author of Maranatha, a Bible study program designed for youth evangelism that has had global outreach. For two years he was a pastor in South Dakota, and for the past eleven years has been a hospice chaplain. A graduate of Southern Adventist University and Florida State University, he has been listed in Who's Who Among American Teachers.

Need additional copies?

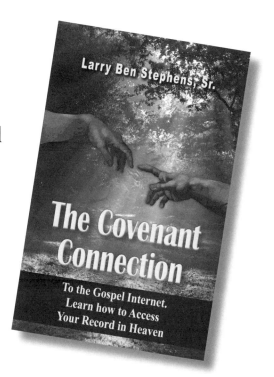

To order more copies of

The Covenant Connection,

contact NewBookPublishing.com

❏ Order online at NewBookPublishing.com

❏ Call 877-311-5100 or

❏ Email Info@NewBookPublishing.com

Call for multiple copy discounts!

ALSO OFFERED
BY LARRY STEPHENS

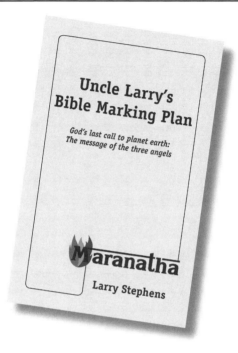

To order your own copy of
Uncle Larry's Bible Marking Plan,
contact NewBookPublishing.com

☐ Order online at:
NewBookPublishing.com/Bookstore

☐ Call 877-311-5100 or

☐ Email Info@NewBookPublishing.com

Call for multiple copy discounts!